THE DEPARTMENT HEAD'S GUIDE TO ASSESSMENT IMPLEMENTATION IN ADMINISTRATIVE AND EDUCATIONAL SUPPORT UNITS

By the same authors

A Practitioner's Handbook for Institutional Effectiveness and Student Outcomes Assessment Implementation

Assessment Case Studies: Common Issues in Implementation with Various Approaches to Resolution

The Departmental Guide and Record Book for Student Outcomes Assessment and Institutional Effectiveness

THE DEPARTMENT HEAD'S GUIDE TO ASSESSMENT IMPLEMENTATION IN ADMINISTRATIVE AND EDUCATIONAL SUPPORT UNITS

by
Karen W. Nichols
Executive Director, Institutional Effectiveness Associates

and

James O. Nichols
Director, University Planning and Institutional Research, University of Mississippi

AGATHON PRESS
New York

© 2000 by Karen W. Nichols and James O. Nichols

AGATHON PRESS
5648 Riverdale Avenue
Bronx, NY 10471

Library of Congress Cataloging-in Publication Data
Nichols, Karen W.
    The department head's guide to assessment implementation in adminis-
trative and educational support units/ by Karen W. Nichols and James O.
Nichols.
    p. cm.
  ISBN 0-87586-130-X
        1. Universities and colleges--United States--Administration--Evaluation--
Handbooks, manuals, etc. 2. Universities and colleges--Employees--Rating of--
United States--Handbooks, manuals, etc. 3. Departmental chairmen (Universi-
ties)--United States--Handbooks, manuals, etc. I. Nichols, James O. (James
Oliver), 1941-II. Title

LB2341 .N46 2000
378.1'01--dc21   00-033151

CONTENTS

FIGURES

PREFACE

On any campus there are several entities involved with the implementation of institutional effectiveness. These entities are: (a) the Chief Executive Officer, (b) the individual or group charged by the Chief Executive Officer with the responsibility for implementation, and (c) the instructional departments as well as administrative and educational support (AES) units where implementation will actually take place. Chief Executive Officers, given their other responsibilities, can reasonably be expected to do no more than understand the importance of institutional effectiveness, give their active support to the process, and provide the resources to see that the job gets done. The individual or group given responsibility for implementation on campus can be expected to organize and support the process. However, the majority of the actual work in implementation of institutional effectiveness will take place within the institution's instructional as well as administrative and educational support (AES) units.

A Practitioner's Handbook for Institutional Effectiveness and Student Outcomes Assessment is intended to be a working reference for that individual or group on the campus charged by the Chief Executive Officer with responsibility for implementation of institutional effectiveness. *A Practitioner's Handbook* provides a generic model for implementation of institutional effectiveness as well as resource sections containing detailed information regarding essential components of the implementation process. *Assessment Case Studies* relates the manner in which eleven institutions, relatively mature in the implementation process, dealt with common issues encountered in implementation from the institutional to the departmental levels.

The third edition of *The Departmental Guide and Record Book for Student Outcomes Assessment and Institutional Effectiveness*, published concurrently with this document, has been refined and refocused to focus solely upon assessment activities within the instructional department. This *Department Head's Guide to Assessment Implementation in Administrative and Educational Support Units* is designed to assist busy AES unit heads that suddenly find themselves dealing with assessment issues which they had not heretofore expected. Its need was clearly identified in assessment case studies and reinforced in the authors' experience as consultants. Over the last ten years, the three earlier publications in this series, *The Practitioner's Handbook, Assessment Case Studies, and the Departmental Guide and Record Book* have more than 30,000 copies. It is anticipated that *The Department Head's Guide to Assessment Implementation in Administrative and Educational Support Units* will round out this complementary and cross-referenced set of guides for implementation of institutional effectiveness within higher education.

The Department Head's Guide to Assessment Implementation in Administrative and Educational Support Units is not meant to be a scholarly work; references are included in only those few instances in which not to do so would border upon plagiarism. It is intended as a document that can be reviewed quickly by the reader who has little time for (or perhaps interest in) assessment theory, but is required to guide implementation within the department/unit.

Over the last dozen years, the authors have assisted more than 250 institutions from major research universities to two-year colleges in the implementation of institutional effectiveness. During the course of that service, discussions with administrative and educational support (AES) departmental administrators/heads have brought forth a relatively consistent series of issues or questions requiring resolution by departmental administrators on each campus in the course of implementation. This experience, actually working with departmental administrators implementing institutional effectiveness, has formed the basis for the material contained in *The Department Head's Guide to Assessment Implementation in Administrative and Educational Support Units*. The authors have sought to keep this publication as simple, focused, and practical as possible in response to urgings from the numerous staff with whom they have worked.

If implementation activities on campus are to be successful, there is no doubt that the Chief Executive Officer must support such action and that the individual or group charged with responsibility for the effort must function effectively. However, equally as important (many would say more important) is the role of the departmental or unit administrator in implementation. Institutional effectiveness is not possible on a campus without successful implementation within instructional programs and AES units. *The Department Head's Guide to Assessment Implementation in Administrative and Educational Support Units* is intended to assist those staff charged with this responsibility.

Karen W. Nichols, James O. Nichols
May 2000

UNDERSTANDING THE REQUIREMENTS FOR ASSESSMENT OR INSTITUTIONAL EFFECTIVENESS IMPLEMENTATION

When Did The Assessment Movement Originate and How Has It Developed?

The assessment movement originated during the early 1980s from a number of national commissions or committees and their reports (*A Nation at Risk: The Imperative for Educational Reform*—Bennett 1983, *Involvement in Learning: Realizing the Potential in American Higher Education*—National Institute for Education, 1984, etc.) which called for reform of higher education, centered on assessment of student learning outcomes.

The federal government (in particular under the tenure of Dr. William Bennett as Secretary of Education) quickly adopted this focus upon educational outcomes as the cornerstone of its changes in policies related to recognition of regional accrediting agencies. These policies, effective in 1987, required regional accrediting agencies to measure the effectiveness of their institutions in terms of:

• Existence of an institutional purpose appropriate for higher education
• Determining that the institution had educational objectives consistent with its mission or purpose
• Documentation of the achievement of students in relation to the intended educational outcomes identified
• Determination of the extent to which institutions regularly evaluate student academic achievement and use its results for improvement of educational programs

This interest in assessment activities extended well through the Bush Administration and has been reflected in various actions taken by the federal government during both of President Clinton's terms in office.

Regional accrediting associations (who play the "Gatekeeper" role in recognition of an institution for the purpose of its students receiving federal financial aid) implemented these requirements within a broad context of institutional expectations which include determination that an institution:

- Has appropriate purposes
- Has the resources needed to accomplish its purposes
- Can demonstrate that it is accomplishing its purposes
- Can give reason to believe that it will continue to accomplish its purposes

Within this general framework, the Commission on Colleges, Southern Association of Colleges and Schools, was the first to require institutional effectiveness implementation on its campuses. It included this requirement in its substantially revised and strengthened, *Criteria for Accreditation,* published originally in 1987. The order of the other regional accrediting associations' integration of the outcomes assessment requirement by the federal government into their expectations for institutions took place in essentially two waves of implementation. During the early 1990s, the North Central Association of Colleges and Schools and the Middle States Association of Colleges and Schools began actively to implement assessment requirements in their publications and campus visitations. During the middle to latter 1990s, the Western Association of Colleges and Schools, Northwest Association of Colleges and Schools, and New England Association of Schools and Colleges became more active in their expectations regarding implementation of institutional effectiveness or assessment activities on campuses which they review.

Paralleling developments at the federal level and their implementation by the regional accrediting associations, assessment initiatives relating to performance funding for institutional accountability were initiated by many state governments. The earliest examples of this were found in performance funding initiatives in the State of Tennessee. The most recent, and some would say controversial, implementation has been that performance funding initiative designed to allocate 100 percent of state support for higher education to institutions in the State of South Carolina based upon their "performance."

What Are Various Assessment Initiatives Seeking to Determine?

While there are differences in terminology between regional accrediting associations and state accountability initiatives, all of these requirements can be described in terms of the institutional effectiveness paradigm shown in Figure 1. The paradigm is composed of three tracks—the educational process, administrative and educational support services, as well as research and public service. Implementation activities regarding these latter two tracks (administrative and educational support as well as research and public service) are described in this publication. While the paradigm shown is explained in considerably more detail in *A Practitioner's Handbook*, it is composed of an Expanded Institutional Statement of Purpose; Intended Educational (student), Research and Public Service Outcomes, as well as Administrative Objectives; Assessment Activities; and Use of Results to Make Program and Service Improvements.

The Expanded Statement of Institutional Purpose (ESIP) is described in the resource section entitled, "Developing the Expanded Statement of Institutional Pur-

Figure 1

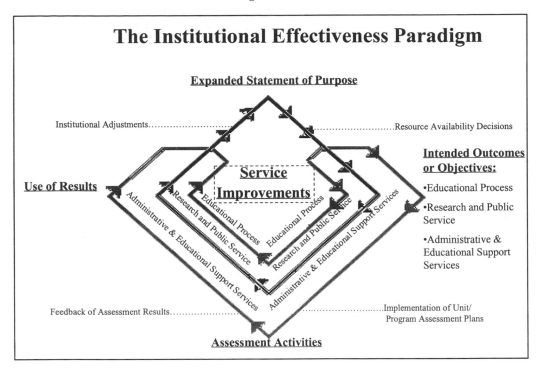

The Institutional Effectiveness Paradigm

pose" in *A Practitioner's Handbook*. The ESIP is composed of a mission statement for the institution, as well as a series of institutional goals. It is often in conjunction with these institutional goals that administrative and educational support units become most involved in the process.

Next, each administrative and educational support unit (AES), as well as each academic program, is required to identify that which it intends to accomplish in support of the Expanded Statement of Institutional Purpose. In this publication, support of the ESIP by AES units, as well as the research and public service units of the institution, will be described as being accomplished through the establishment of "administrative objectives." While the primary focus of assessment activity remains upon an institution's instructional programs, both administrative and educational support units are also included in order to have a comprehensive institutional effectiveness program. These units might otherwise not have expected to participate in the assessment of their services because of the emphasis on student outcomes.

Following identification of administrative and educational support "administrative objectives," units are asked to assess or measure the extent to which these objectives are being met. In administrative and educational support units, that measurement often takes place in terms of client satisfaction, external evaluations, or relatively simple direct measures of unit performance and assessment of student outcomes following receipt of service. The third chapter of this publication, "Preparing the Assessment Plan," contains a description of how to go about identification of administrative objectives and means of assessment for those objectives. These components taken together constitute the "Assessment Plan" for each administrative and educational support unit.

After the actual conduct of assessment activities, each AES unit is called upon to use the results to improve its *services* to students or other clientele. The accomplishment of assessment activities, the description of the use of results, and the documentation of the use of those results are included in Chapter Four, "From Planning to Implementation and Use of Results."

Taken as a whole, the completed institutional effectiveness paradigm from statement of purpose through administrative objectives, assessment activities, and use of results to improve services, is described in the jargon of this field as "Closing of the Loop." It is this "Closing of the Loop" (through use of results) that is becoming the primary expectation of regional accreditation agencies.

What Is the Future of the Assessment Movement?

Based upon the growing expectations of regional accrediting agencies, there is no doubt that the requirement for institutions to demonstrate comprehensively (though assessment activities) that they are effective is spreading progressively across the rest of the country during the next three to five years. Those institutions in the Southern, North Central and Middle States accrediting association regions already clearly understand the importance of this subject. Those in the Western, Northwest, and New England accrediting association regions can expect to feel the escalation of institutional effectiveness expectations most acutely during this period of time.

If past patterns of implementation hold constant, institutions in the first wave of implementation (Southern, North Central, and Middle States accrediting associations) can anticipate the requirement for complete and comprehensive implementation (through use of results) in all educational programs during the next several years. Those institutions located in the second wave of implementation (Western, Northwestern, and New England accrediting associations) should expect requirements for "Assessment Plans" throughout the next several years leading to full campus implementation and use of results within five years.

The other major development in assessment expectations during the foreseeable future will be the growing inclusion of administrative and educational units. These units will be required to demonstrate assessment activities leading to improvements in their services. Chapter Two documents specific expectations regarding this requirement by regional accrediting associations as of fall 1999. Further expansion into administrative and educational support and administrative services can be expected to continue throughout the next three to five years.

CHAPTER II

INTRODUCTION TO ASSESSMENT IN ADMINISTRATIVE AND EDUCATIONAL SUPPORT (AES) UNITS

Why Am I Participating in the Assessment Activities at Our Institution?

The *reason* Administrative and Educational Support (AES) units are asked to take part in assessment activities is in order to provide information through which they can improve their services. The *occasion* for this "request" is frequently connected with their institutions reaffirmation of accreditation.

Many administrative and educational support department heads assume assessment activities on their campus are exclusively the pleasure of those engaged with the instructional program at the institution. However, all regional accrediting associations require, in one way or another, that the institution show that its statement of purpose or mission is being accomplished. While the major portion of this "accomplishment" takes place in instructional programs, some portions of the statement of purpose (particularly institutional goals) usually also relate to administrative and educational support units. This requirement that the institution demonstrate and document that it is accomplishing its statement of purpose or mission is described by most regional accreditation requirements as "Institutional Effectiveness."

The extent to which documented evidence is required of this *formal* AES unit support of the institutional statement of purpose varies substantially by regional accreditation agencies. The Commission on Colleges, Southern Association of Colleges and Schools (SACS), explicitly charges administrative and educational support units in its *Criteria for Accreditation* with the accomplishment of assessment activities and use of the results for the improvement of services which are linked to and directly support the institutional statement of purpose. In most other regional accrediting associations, the requirement for involvement of administrative and educational support units in support of the statement of purpose and assessment activities is more implicit or limited in scope, usually referring to co-curricular, student life, library services, and information technology, supporting the instructional component of the institution. The requirements of each regional accrediting agency regarding assessment in administrative and educational support services are illustrated in Figure 2.

Figure 2

Citations Regarding Regional Accrediting Association Requirements for Administrative and Educational Support (AES)Units

Commission on Colleges, Southern Association of Colleges and Schools, *Criteria for Accreditation*, **1998**

3.2 Planning and Evaluation: Administrative and Educational Support Services
   In addition to providing evidence of planning and evaluation in its educational program, the institution must demonstrate planning and evaluation in its administrative and educational support services. For each administrative and educational support service unit, the institution must:
   1. establish a clearly defined purpose which supports the institution's purpose and goals
   2. formulate goals which support the purpose of each unit
   3. develop and implement procedures to evaluate the extent to which these goals are being achieved in each unit
   4. use the results of the evaluations to improve administrative and educational support services.

   Each unit, in its planning and evaluation processes, should consider internal and external factors and develop evaluation methods which will yield information useful to the planning processes of that unit.

Commission on Institutions of Higher Education, North Central Association of Colleges and Schools, *Handbook of Accreditation,* **1997**

   "…evaluation of overall institutional effectiveness is dependent upon the institution's documentation of how well it is accomplishing not only its educational purposes, but also all other purposes and objectives needed in order to fulfill its mission."

Commission on Higher Education, Middle States Association of Colleges and Schools, *Framework for Assessment*, **Second Edition**

Personal and Social Development
   Institutional statements about the goals of higher education almost always include aspects of personality and character as well as intellect. Although most agree that affective outcomes are derived from virtually all forms of student involvement with the institution, outcomes relating to student development ordinarily are associated with the "co-curriculum."
   The "co-curriculum" consists of out-of-class activities that are organized to supplement the classroom curriculum as well as educational offerings for which students do not receive credit or which are not required for graduation. It includes advising, tutoring, counseling, financial aid, study facilities, discipline, health, government, athletics, student-faculty-administrative relations, clubs, and other out-of-class activities.

Accrediting Commission for Senior Colleges and Universities, Western Association of Schools and Colleges, *Handbook of Accreditation*, **1997**

   As an essential element in planning and evaluating institutional effectiveness, institutional research is conducted. Research assesses such elements as instructional programs, research functions, and the co-curricular environment.
   Institutions with research and public service missions assess the extent to which support is provided and activities undertaken to accomplish these aspects of their mission.

Figure 2 (continued)

Accrediting Commission for Community and Junior Colleges, Western Association of Schools and Colleges, *Standards for Accreditation,* **1999**

The institution systematically evaluates the appropriateness, adequacy, and effectiveness of its student services and uses the results of the evaluation as a basis for improvement.

The institution plans for and systematically evaluates the adequacy and effectiveness of its learning and information resources and services and makes appropriate changes as necessary.

Commission on Colleges, Northwest Association of Schools and Colleges, *Accreditation Handbook,* **1999**

Related evaluation and processes regularly assess the quality, accessibility, and use of libraries and other information resource repositories and their services to determine the level of effectiveness in support of the educational program.

Commission on Institutions of Higher Education, Northeast Association of Colleges and Schools, *Standards for Accreditation,* **1992**

Through a program of regular and systematic evaluation, the institution determines whether the co-curricular goals and needs of the students are being met. Information obtained through this evaluation is used to revise these goals and improve their achievement.

The institution regularly and systematically evaluates the adequacy and utilization of its library and information resources, and uses the results of the data to improve and increase the effectiveness of these services.

In addition to regional accreditation, many AES units are engaged in assessment activity as part of intrinsically motivated attempts to improve services through Total Quality Management (TQM) or Continuance Quality Improvement (CQI) initiatives. The relationship of Total Quality Management and Continuance Quality Improvement initiatives to assessment activities designed to satisfy regional accrediting associations is described later in this chapter.

How Does Assessment of Institutional Effectiveness Relate to the Strategic Planning Already Taking Place on Many Campuses?

On many campuses both strategic planning and institutional effectiveness or assessment planning are conducted. They are necessary and often required by regional accrediting associations. However, they are different in their approach to planning and it is vitally important that institutions recognize and respect the different purposes which each serves (see Figure 3).

Strategic planning on campuses is frequently a product of presidential leadership or the requirements of the governing board. Regional accrediting associations also often require some form of strategic planning activity. Such planning focuses upon the question, "What actions should we take to implement the Expanded Statement of Institutional Purpose?" As such, strategic planning often results in a series of action

Figure 3

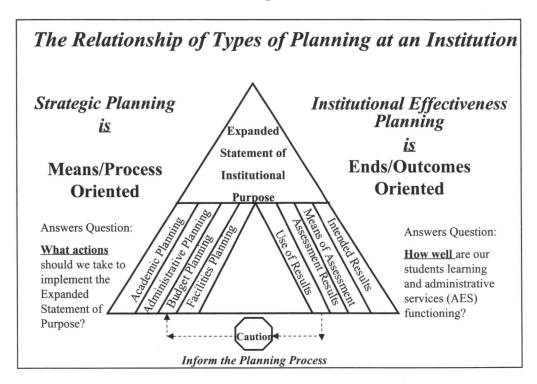

plans (these are frequently long range) with resource requirements to put into action the necessary *processes* to accomplish the statement of purpose. Strategic planning is characterized by:

- Administrative planning
- Fiscal planning
- Physical facilities planning
- Budget planning

In AES units, such administrative planning often focuses on the *means* through which to improve processes or make the unit's operations more *efficient*. These administrative planning efforts often include cross training of staff, improving communications with other administrative offices, and implementation of improved record-keeping activities. It is only after these administrative planning activities have been accomplished and are part of the services provided by the unit, that they are subject to assessment regarding the extent to which they are *effective* in providing services to the unit's clients which is the *end* result sought.

Strategic planning takes place in order for an institution to survive and/or go about its development and refinement. A number of institutions has assumed that since strategic planning was being well accomplished on the campus, then institutional effectiveness planning was also being accomplished. The negative findings regarding effectiveness planning by regional accrediting association reaffirmation visitation committees resulting from this assumption have been a shock to many of these institutions.

Institutional effectiveness planning also relates to the statement of purpose for the institution. However, it asks the basic question, "How well are our students learning and administrative (AES) services functioning?" Thus, institutional effectiveness planning is very *ends* or *outcomes* oriented and focuses upon the results of the institution's efforts (as opposed to the efforts or processes implemented) as measured by services provided by AES units and student learning in instructional programs. Institutional effectiveness planning is characterized by:

- Expected results (administrative objectives)
- Means of assessment
- Actual assessment results
- The use of results to improve services

If We're Doing Strategic Planning, Isn't That Enough?

Both strategic planning and institutional effectiveness planning are necessary for a campus to be in compliance with most regional accreditation requirements. The danger is that, because of the prior existence of strategic planning activities, institutions often do not implement institutional effectiveness planning activities until after being scourged by their regional accrediting association.

Certainly, the strategic action plans resulting from administrative and educational support unit administrative planning may cause an increase in requests for provision of resources with which to offer services (personnel, better equipment, office supplies, etc.) being requested or provided. However, if an institution attempts to "assess" the accomplishment of its strategic action plans, it determines:

- Were the personnel provided?
- Was the equipment purchased?
- Were there enough office supplies?
- Was the new form implemented?

This focus is altogether insufficient and differs from the institutional effectiveness or ends focused assessment of the *results* of these activities or:

- Measures of increased client satisfaction
- Direct measures of increased levels of service
- Validation of services by external reviews
- Ability of the client after receiving service

Units' strategic action or administrative plans include descriptions of services which the unit believes will be improved as a result of changes in an AES unit process. These administrative planning activities such as "implementing an on-line transcript service" or "designing an improved inventory check list" are found on the left side (strategic planning side) of the triangle shown in Figure 3. When the unit is preparing administrative objectives for institutional effectiveness (found on the right side of the triangle shown in Figure 3), seldom do they include such administrative planning initiatives describing processes to be improved.

While many of the regional accrediting associations support the use of assessment results in institutional planning and budgeting, in the authors' opinion, if assessment activities are identified widely on the campus as the means through which to justify or drive budget requests, the use of these assessment results for service improvement will substantially diminish. However, from a conceptual standpoint, use of assessment results to impact resource allocation and budgeting is very attractive. From a practical standpoint, it undermines the process of program or service improvement in several ways. First, if assessment results are seen primarily as justification for the request of additional resources, then the absence of additional resources will be widely utilized as a reason for not making service improvements. Under these circumstances, many AES units will never stop to consider what improvements could be made within existing unit resources, but will move directly to requests for additional resources which in many institutions stand little chance of funding. Second, in some AES units the means of assessment and criteria for success will be crafted in such a way as to justify a request for additional resources rather than improve services. Third, both of the previously described circumstances will lead rapidly toward staff consideration of assessment as a means through which to "play the game," rather than genuinely improve services offered. AES units are urged to exercise caution in the use of assessment results as a justification for requesting additional resources. Rather, AES units need to first ask, "Given the personnel and resources we currently have, how can our unit improve its services?"

So, the answer to the question is simply, if you're doing strategic planning which results in unit action plans, etc., that is probably not sufficient to meet requirements concerning institutional effectiveness and the improvement of services by educational support and administrative units.

What Types of Administrative and Educational Support (AES) Units Are We Talking About?

This publication addresses assessment implementation in the "non-instructional" components of the institution. *The Department Head's Guide* includes a description of assessment activities in both more traditional administrative and educational support (AES) units, as well as separate chapters regarding assessment in organized research units and service/continuing education activities.

Administrative units provide services which maintain the institution and are essential to its operations, but do not impact directly the institution's instructional programs. Examples of such units include the Accounting Office, the Office of the Registrar, Physical Plant Department, and other such essential units.

On the other hand, **educational support units** are those which, while not primarily instructional in nature, contribute directly to student learning or instruction. Examples of educational support units include: Academic Advising Center, Library, and Information Technology. Each of these units focuses upon providing services, which directly relate to the students and, in many cases, are part of the institution's overall learning environment or process.

One of the first issues to be settled at any institution involved in assessment within administrative and educational support (AES) units is the identification of the *"units"* to take part. Fortunately, there is a large amount of flexibility provided by regional accrediting associations regarding the structure of assessment activities in AES units. The institution's choices are basically two in its identification of "units":

- At larger institutions with more fully developed AES organizational structures, the term "unit" is normally equated with a "department," having a relatively singular function (Accounting, Career Planning, Alumni Affairs, etc.).
- At smaller institutions, it is often difficult to identify AES units. Many times a number of service areas (organized separately as departments at larger institutions) are housed within one "umbrella" administrative department, such as the Department of Student Services which might include the career planning, personal counseling, financial aid, etc., service areas. Regional accrediting agencies allow institutions to identify their AES units. The authors suggest that this identification process is somewhat eased by determining first, if separate budgetary allocations have been made to each service area within such an "umbrella department" and second, if separate identifiable and distinct services are performed by each service area. If either of these conditions is met (separate budget or distinct services), it is suggested that each service area within an existing "umbrella" department prepare and execute a separate assessment plan as explained later in this publication. The alternative is to prepare one assessment plan for the "umbrella" department, however, each service area within the department should be represented by one or more administrative objectives/means of assessment/use of results.

Two specialized types of educational support units, which differ from most other units previously described, are *separately organized research units* and *service/continuing education activities*. Separately organized research units are those entities, beyond expected levels of faculty departmental research, which are separately organized and often separately funded on a campus. These units typically focus upon research in a specific area such as mineral resources, pharmaceutical sciences, physical acoustics, etc., and are frequently typified by titles such as center or institute. External service/continuing education activities are those separately organized, identified and funded units on a campus which provide direct services (beyond those offered by individual faculty members) over a period of time to clients. Often these services are provided to members of the public having no other connection to the institution. Also included among external services units are those providing (credit and non-credit) continuing education offerings away from the home campus. Examples of external service units include entities providing services concerning speech and hearing, poison control, population demographics, agriculture, home economics, non-credit courses, branch campuses, etc. These external services units are also frequently identified as centers or other similar titles. Chapter Six describes assessment in these types of units in greater detail.

On an increasing number of campuses, administrative services such as the bookstore, food service, and janitorial services have been "out sourced" to private contractors. The institution remains responsible for these services, and hence, the "out sourced" service areas should take part in the same assessment procedures as other AES units.

In summary, early in the process of implementation of assessment activities an institution needs to identify its administrative and educational support (AES) units that will be taking part. This should be accomplished in an organized fashion so that the campus can begin the processes described in the following chapters with a clear sense of structure.

How Does Assessment in Administrative and Educational Support Units Differ From Those Related Activities Taking Place in Our Campus' Instructional Programs and Other Forms of "Evaluation" Already in Place?

Assessment in administrative and educational support units differs from student outcomes assessment, employee evaluation, and Total Quality Management/Continuous Quality Improvement initiatives, as well as Re-engineering projects in a number of important ways.

The primary difference between student outcomes assessment, as practiced in instructional programs, and assessment in AES units relates to the focus of the expected results. In the instructional aspect of the institution, expected results are focused upon educational or student outcomes, what the *graduates* or *students* will be able to think, know, or do when they have completed their program. Statements related to each instructional program's intended results lend themselves to this focus and *statements of what the faculty or departments intend to do themselves are not allowed.*

On the other hand, within administrative and educational support units, statements regarding what services the *unit intends* to accomplish *are entirely acceptable since many of these units are removed from direct contact with the learning environment.* Objectives for administrative units consist primarily of such "process oriented" statements describing the support process or service which the unit intends to accomplish. Typical of such *process oriented* statements of administrative objectives are the following:

- Improve services to handicapped students
- Monthly accounting reports to academic and administrative departments will be processed and distributed promptly
- Transcript requests will be filled and returned promptly

However, those statements of administrative objectives from such educational support units as the Library, Career Services, Information Technology, etc., frequently contain both "process" and "student outcomes" oriented objectives. These *outcomes oriented* objectives concern these units' direct impact upon students or clients served. They describe what the client will be able to do after receipt of the services provided by the educational support unit. Examples of such outcomes oriented objectives from educational support units include the following:

- Students will be able to utilize the library's reference services efficiently
- Before their last semester in attendance at the institution, graduates seeking employment will prepare an acceptable resume for presentation to potential employers
- Students will be proficient in logging on to the Internet through the academic computing center

In addition to this primary difference in the types of statements being assessed, AES unit assessment activities differ from those being practiced in the instructional portion of the institution in (a) the limited types of assessment activities normally utilized, (b) the speed of implementation and (c) the degree of staff acceptance. Each of these is discussed in greater detail in later chapters.

Assessment *for effectiveness* in administrative and educational support units is clearly different than individual employee evaluation. Employee evaluation, an important and legitimate form of activity on our campuses, is focused upon the individual and, to a large extent, is summative in nature. As such, it focuses upon judgments concerning an individual's performance and, on occasion, upon strategies for individual improvement. Assessment activities are focused at the unit level and address improvement of services without judgmental findings regarding individuals.

It is extremely important that this difference between personnel evaluation and assessment in AES units be widely communicated, understood and believed by an institution's administrative staff. If institutional staff believe that the assessment activities in AES units are being utilized to make judgments concerning individuals or the unit, they will naturally structure statements of administrative objectives and identify means of assessment which will reflect favorably upon themselves. This will defeat the purpose of assessment of effectiveness for *ser-*

vice improvement because only those endeavors which need little or no improvement, will be brought forward by the staff involved. It may become necessary for the institution to craft a statement concerning the use of assessment results, clearly separating AES activities from individual personnel evaluation or judgment concerning a unit's worthiness.

Administrative and educational support unit assessment endeavors relate in many ways to Total Quality Management/Continuous Quality Improvement (TQM/CQI) initiatives frequently taking place on campuses. AES assessment and TQM/CQI focus upon the improvement of institutional services and are compatible with one another. On campuses in which TQM/CQI initiatives have been fully and successfully implemented, there is little else that needs to be done in the way of assessment in administrative and educational support units. However, on campuses without such successful TQM/CQI initiatives taking place, the AES assessment procedures described in the following pages can contribute to significant service improvements without the level of effort, or stress frequently associated with TQM/CQI initiatives. AES assessment procedures can also be a logical or reasonable fall-back position which will retain efforts to improve services, should TQM/CQI initiatives prove to be too burdensome to be sustained by an institution over any period of time.

"Re-engineering" is among the current "buzz words" moving through administrative circles in higher education. Various authors describe this process in almost innumerable ways. However, in most cases, the term re-engineering relates to very carefully examining a portion of the institution's administrative processes to include their intent, existing procedures, and results. Following this substantial study, "re-engineering" or changing of the process is brought about. The purpose of this effort is usually described as gaining increased efficiency.

AES assessment activities differ from re-engineering in several important ways. First, the basic unit of analysis or study in AES assessment is the unit, whereas the administrative process (which may cut across several units) is the focus of re-engineering. Second, AES assessment engages the entire administrative and educational support structure of an institution at one time with all units participating in a recurring cycle. Re-engineering projects most frequently deal with only one segment of the institution's administrative processes at a time. Third, AES improvement activities in most units focus on the fine tuning or incremental improvement of services based upon existing staff and procedures. In re-engineering, administrative processes are identified and carefully studied in great detail because of their ultimate importance to the institution rather than their current perceived lack of effectiveness, efficiency, or client satisfaction. Re-engineering procedures lead to the detailed analysis of *all portions of the process* selected and often result in substantial (as opposed to incremental) change in procedures. Fourth, re-engineering efforts are frequently accompanied by claims of dramatic increases in *efficiency* brought about by reductions in cost (manpower). AES assessment activities, on the other hand, are focused primarily on increasing or improving services (*effectiveness*) within existing manpower and resources, rather than improving efficiency.

It is important to understand these differences to be able to deal with misgivings on the part of employees. Each procedure (AES assessment, personnel evaluations, TQM/CQI and re-engineering) is appropriate should an institution choose to implement it. However, they are each relatively different from one another, having different purposes, and often different results on the campus.

What Is the Institutional Context for Assessment in Administrative and Educational Support (AES) Units?

There are seldom circumstances under which assessment activities will be initiated in administrative and educational support units without being part of an overall program of assessment activities (often described as institutional effectiveness) being undertaken by the entire institution. A campus is normally undertaking such a broad institutional assessment initiative in order to demonstrate the use of assessment results to improve the services provided students and their improved learning, in response to a requirement by regional accrediting associations. While the nature and extent of AES unit involvement in this overall institutional effort to demonstrate improvement in services varies from one regional accrediting association to another (see Figure 2, page 16), all aspects of the institution are expected to be able to demonstrate their support to the institution's statement of purpose at the time of the visiting team's review.

Individual AES units should know what other AES units and instructional programs are doing regarding assessment as well as what institutional support is available for assessment activities of their own unit. As part of an overall institutional effectiveness implementation, many campuses provide educational opportunities such as seminars or workshops for faculty and staff initiating assessment activities. Because of the differences in approach ("outcomes" vs. "process" orientation) between instructional programs and AES units, the authors have prepared this publication as well as the third edition of *The Departmental Guide and Record Book for Student Outcomes Assessment and Institutional Effectiveness* now available from Agathon Press. Likewise, separate workshops and/or seminars need to be conducted for each group (instructional faculty and AES staff) on each campus. Attempts to combine seminars or workshops for both instructional faculty and AES staff frequently result in boredom on the part of both groups of participants as the part of assessment related to the "other component" is presented. Also, confusion as to what assessment procedures are appropriate in each sphere (instructional and AES) frequently develops.

Often, campuses establish institution-wide control or coordination measures and procedures for assessment activities. Individual AES units should seek to determine the existence of an institutional timeline or dates by which various assessment activities are expected to transpire. They should determine whether a common reporting procedure for documentation purposes (such as that described in Appendix A) has been adopted. They need to be familiar with what other AES assessment units are doing. Frequently, there is no better way to "get started" than to visit or study another AES unit providing related services that has been successful in its implementation of assessment and improvement procedures.

Each AES unit should also determine what assessment support from the institutional level is available for conducting assessment activities concerning the unit. The institution should have conducted an inventory of existing assessment activities which the AES unit can utilize in making this determination. This support is often in the form of survey research related to client satisfaction measures. The unit should identify existing institutional level questionnaires or surveys of graduating students, alumni, etc., to determine if satisfaction measures regarding the specific services provided by the unit are being asked of the respondents. Both of the authors frequently discover that client satisfaction measures regarding AES units are being conducted at the institutional level and by other units; however, the results of those surveys are not being distributed to the individual AES units. If institutional level measures of client satisfaction with AES services have indeed been taking place, each AES unit should seek to identify the results to date as soon as possible. In many cases, locally developed institutional level questionnaire items regarding client satisfaction with AES services will need to be adapted to better fit specific administrative objectives identified by the individual AES units.

In addition to the utilization of institutional level questionnaires for assessment purposes within individual AES units, many institutions provide services to facilitate design, production, processing, and analysis of in-depth survey research connected with assessment of specific procedures. It is not uncommon for survey research facilities utilizing automated survey processing support packages to be provided to assist individual AES units in conducting the client satisfaction research described later in Chapter Three. This service is usually housed in the institutional research component on each campus. However, individual AES units can expect that they will probably be held responsible for the distribution of the surveys to the respondents and may be asked to coordinate or time their survey activities so as not to duplicate other units. They may also be asked to bear the "out-of-pocket" costs for such surveys.

AES unit department heads can also gain valuable assessment information from institutional level activities such as the National Association of College and University Business Officers (NACUBO) Benchmarking study taking place on some campuses. This study was launched in 1991 for the purpose of providing an organized forum for institutions to identify opportunities to improve operating efficiencies and effectiveness. The program provides hard data for self-analysis of forty functional areas related to administrative and educational support services and is also described further in Chapter Three. While participation in the NACUBO Benchmarking program is not a substitute for AES unit assessment implementation, data potentially useful in AES unit assessment operations can be gleaned from this type of source.

While each AES unit may initially feel alone in implementation, that is not the case. The more the unit can learn about what is expected by the institution, what others are doing, and what help is available, the easier implementation will become.

Who Should Be Involved in Implementation of Assessment Within Administrative and Educational Support Units?

The question of involvement in AES unit assessment implementation is key to long-term successful implementation within such units. The AES unit director or head, professional staff, and the unit supervisor all can make important contributions to successful implementation. Just as easily, the action of these individuals or groups can substantially impede successful implementation.

The AES unit department head (director) is perhaps the most important ingredient in successful assessment implementation. The role of AES unit department heads is to lead their staff in assessment planning, implementation, and service improvement. AES department heads will undoubtedly be charged with submission of assessment plans for their units. They must act expeditiously, resist procrastination, and avoid closing their office door and emerging with the AES unit assessment plan without the participation of their staff. Some regional accrediting associations specify the importance of staff involvement in the assessment process. If the assessment plan is solely the product of the unit head, many of the unit staff will be pleased by not being bothered with involvement in preparation and the unit's supervisor will have the required assessment plan. This apparent success will be short lived. When unit staff are later asked to take part in implementation of the means of assessment identified, they will begin to *question* (openly or not) the reasons for specific assessment efforts causing them more work and will be much less likely to use the results to make changes designed to improve unit services. The point is AES unit department heads need to *lead* their staff in this effort from its inception, if they expect the staff's commitment at the conclusion.

Clearly, the professional staff in each AES unit should take part in identifying and selecting administrative objectives as described, as well as the means of assessment and criteria for success described in Chapter Three. These professional level staff are, in most cases, directly or indirectly engaged in managing the services of the unit. Failure to include them in this process from its inception would be a serious impediment to successful implementation.

The extent of involvement of clerical level staff in implementation will vary depending on the unit and to some extent the campus. Within larger AES units, typically found on those campuses with enrollment above 7,500 students, initial involvement of clerical staff is less frequent. Whereas, on smaller campuses where AES units are of more modest size, involvement of clerical staff early in the process is far more common. At a very minimum on either type of campus, unit clerical staff should have an opportunity to review, comment upon, and make suggestions for potential change in administrative objectives as well as means of assessment and criteria for success before they are finalized by the unit. Involving clerical staff contributes to a cohesive understanding of unit assessment activities. It is important to remember that these clerical staff will be expected to implement many of the service improvements which will ultimately result from assessment findings and that if they are going to be committed to the improvement process at that time, they need to be equally committed to the assessment process as it is designed and implemented.

The supervisor to whom the unit reports, frequently at the vice presidential level, has an important role to play in assessment activities as well. The supervisor to whom the unit reports should be indirectly involved in the preparation of administrative objectives, means of assessment and criteria for success and use of results. This involvement should include approval or adjustment of the unit's assessment plan, review of its results, and acknowledgment of the unit's on going efforts toward self-improvement. Rather than controlling unit assessment activities, the unit's supervisor should attempt to create a supporting environment for assessment resulting in the encouragement or "coaching" of his subordinate's assessment initiatives leading toward service improvement. Attempts to control or dictate assessment policies by the unit's supervisor will result in justifiable concerns that the process is being used not for self-improvement, but in order to make judgments concerning AES unit performance and personnel.

In most cases, the AES unit supervisors will be asked to ensure that their units are taking part in assessment activities in order to comply with campus wide institutional effectiveness requirements. Therefore, AES unit supervisors should be kept *informed* of developments within each unit reporting to them and should be expected to take the necessary action to see that the self-improvement initiatives inherent within assessment activities are taking place in their support units.

What Components Should Be Included in the Completed AES Unit Assessment/ Improvement Report?

The balance of this monograph is directed toward implementation in each administrative and educational support unit of the components identified in the Office of the Registrar, Five-Column Model shown in Figure 4. These components include:

* Reference to the institution's missions and goals (statement of purpose) and its support by the unit's mission statement
* Formulation of administrative objectives
* Identification of means of assessment and criteria for success for each administrative objective
* Summary of the data actually collected when the planned assessment took place
* Description of how these data were used to improve services

Each of these components will be explained in greater detail in the following chapters. Finally, documentation of these assessment activities is explained in Chapter Five.

How Do We Go About Implementing the Concepts Illustrated in Figure 4?

The balance of this monograph is organized around the Suggested Steps for Administrative Assessment Process depicted in Figure 5. These steps are designed to facilitate the implementation of the concepts included in the "Five-Column Model" illustrated in Figure 4.

The first four steps indicated in Figure 5 constitute the formulation of the unit assessment plan and lead each unit through the first three columns of the "Five-Column Model" shown in Figure 4. In the fifth and sixth steps, the unit moves from planning its assessment activities to actual implementation of those activities and "Closing the Loop" or use of the results to improve services. These last two steps cover the fourth and fifth columns of the "Five-Column Model" referenced. In each of the following chapters, the steps are fully explained and examples provided. It is essential that the steps be followed *in order* to prevent unnecessary assessment activities and disappointment on the part of those responsible for implementation.

What Is a Reasonable Amount of Time for Implementation of Assessment Activities in AES Units?

There is nothing described in the following pages, which cannot be accomplished with modest effort in the space of twelve months. In practice, many AES units are able to move much quicker to complete implementation based upon already existing procedures and means of assessment. Figure 6 provides a generic timeline assuming an administrative or educational support unit begins implementation at the beginning of the fall semester and has done no previous work in this area.

Figure 6 suggests formulation of the unit's assessment plan during the fall semester, conducting assessment activities throughout the spring semester, and concludes with the use of results and documentation before classes begin the next fall semester. These periods of time are rather generous and should facilitate accomplishment by AES units with minimal disruption of services.

Implementation of the timeline shown in Figure 6 should require no more than several days of time spread over the twelve-month period. Senior staff (the department head and professional staff) will assume leadership roles while AES staff should provide input and in many cases will be directly involved in implementation of the means of assessment identified, and the improvement of services.

Conclusion

This chapter has provided a general framework, including a conceptual model for implementation of assessment activities in AES units as well as the components necessary in assessment activities within each unit. On a more practical basis, it has

Figure 4

Office of the Registrar
Five-Column Model

Institutional Mission/Goals Reference / Unit Mission Statement	Administrative Objectives	Means of Assessment & Criteria for Success	Summary of Data Collected	Use of Results
Institutional Mission/Goals Reference Goal #4: To assist students in achieving their educational goals by making available quality student and educational support services.	1. Increase student satisfaction with the overall registration process.	1a. Responses on the Graduating Student Survey related to "overall satisfaction with the registration process" will average from 2.7 to 3.5 on a five-point scale.	1a. Response improved to 3.2; however, response of students attending after 7:00 p.m. remained unchanged at 1.9.	1a. Progress noted. Office of the Registrar to remain open until 8:00 p.m. during registration and for first week of class by re-scheduling of employees.
		1b. The number of "complaints" left in the Registrar's "suggestion box" will decrease from an average of 53 each semester to approximately 40. No single area of service will receive more than 1/3 of the suggestions each month.	1b. The number of "complaints" increased to an average of 55. Many of these complaints related to computer response time.	1b. Installation of new hardware should reduce comments next semester.
Unit Mission Statement The Registrar's Office is responsible for processing applications for admission, processing and reporting student enrollment, maintaining registered student records, receiving grades, and the processing of transcript information.	2. Shorten response time for transcript requests.	2a. The average number of days from receipt of transcript requests to posting of response will be reduced from 4.5 to 3.5 days based upon a one week sample taken at random each semester. No transcript request will be found to have longer than five working days.	2a. Average response time for mail requests was 3.3 days during proceeding twelve months. Longest response time found to be 4 1/2 days.	2a. Staff voted to monitor one more year. Records are being kept regarding high demand time for possible shift in personnel.
		2b. "Over the counter" requests for transcripts will be filled within 24 hours as measured one day each month.	2b. During registration and pre-registration, many "over the counter requests" were unfilled after 48 hours.	2b. Staff diversion from transcript request service during registration no longer authorized.
	3. Provide accurate class enrollment data.	3a. Student credit hour auditors from the governing board will verify the accuracy of class enrollments each semester reporting "no adjustments required."	3a. In most recent two audits, class enrollment reporting was verified and "no adjustments required."	3a. Due to importance to institutional formula funding, continue to be monitored.

Figure 5

Suggested Steps for Administrative Assessment Process

Formulating Unit Assessment Plan:

First -   Establish a linkage to the Institution's Statement of Purpose. Identify which portion of the Expanded Statement of Institutional Purpose the AES Unit Supports

Second -   Prepare the AES Unit Mission Statement

Third -   Formulate Administrative Objectives

Fourth-   Identify Unit Means of Assessment and Criteria for Success

Moving from Planning to Implementation and Use of Results:

Fifth -   Conduct Assessment Activities

Sixth -   Document Use of Results for Service Improvements

Figure 6

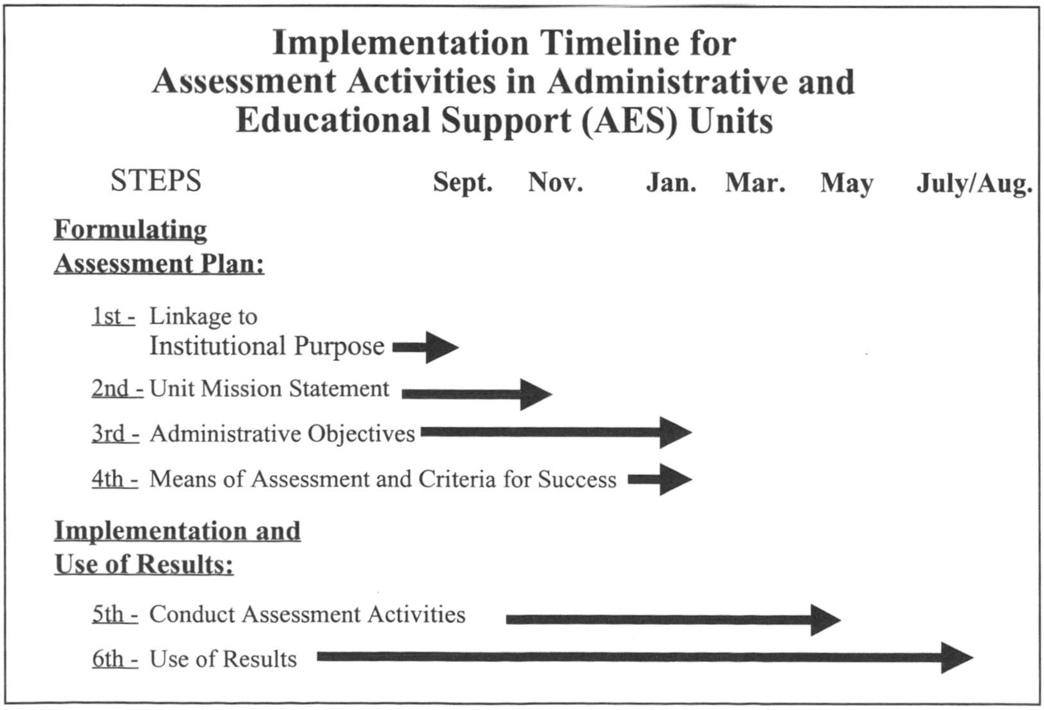

Implementation Timeline for Assessment Activities in Administrative and Educational Support (AES) Units

STEPS	Sept.	Nov.	Jan.	Mar.	May	July/Aug.

Formulating Assessment Plan:

1st - Linkage to Institutional Purpose ➤

2nd - Unit Mission Statement ➤

3rd - Administrative Objectives ➤

4th - Means of Assessment and Criteria for Success ➤

Implementation and Use of Results:

5th - Conduct Assessment Activities ➤

6th - Use of Results ➤

reviewed the types of AES units included, roles of the administrators/staff in implementation, a six-step process for implementation, and an approximate implementation timeline. Specific descriptions and examples of implementation using the six-step process in AES units, very much like your own, are provided in the following chapters.

CHAPTER III

FORMULATING THE UNIT ASSESSMENT PLAN

Just as all of us learned to walk before we learned to run, it is necessary to formulate a unit assessment plan prior to actually doing the assessment and using the results to improve services. Failure to establish a logical and coherent plan for assessment, would have the same results as the infant that attempts to dash across the room before it can toddle from one piece of furniture to another, a resounding fall. It is the authors' experience that far too many AES units begin implementation at the bottom of the paradigm shown in Figure 1 (page 13) by "doing assessment," only to find major portions of their effort wasted and eventually redone. It is far more effective to move through the four steps described in the following sections carefully and methodically in preparing for assessment, than to rush into assessment activities leading frequently to a crash.

STEP ONE—ESTABLISH A LINKAGE TO THE INSTITUTION'S STATEMENT OF PURPOSE

All planning at an institution should support its statement of purpose. This statement of purpose is normally composed of a set of relatively unchanging "truths" about the institution. In many cases, this statement is known as its "mission." The mission describes the enduring nature of the institution and the purpose for its existence. In addition to this institutional mission statement, frequently there appears a number of "institutional goals," which reflect the institution's intentions over a shorter period of time. These institutional goals link to and support the overarching values or "truths" contained in the mission. These two statements, mission and institutional goals, considered together, constitute the overall Expanded Statement of Institutional Purpose for an institution. Means for development of such an Expanded Statement of Institutional Purpose (ESIP) are outlined in *A Practitioner's Handbook for Institutional Effectiveness and Student Outcomes Assessment Implementation*, third edition. (See resource section "Developing the Expanded Statement of Institutional Purpose," by Michael Yost).

Statements of purpose for an institution have gradually changed over the last fifteen to twenty years. Earlier they were characterized as being primarily aspirational in nature and frequently filled with "truth and beauty" rarely attainable. Recently, statements of purpose have become more realistic in terms of what an institution "is" and "can realistically strive to accomplish." Part of this change has been due to changing regional accreditation requirements. These requirements include the need for demonstration of more comprehensive support of the statement of purpose by all the operating units of the institution, including instructional programs, research and public service units as well as the administrative and educational support units to which this monograph is directed.

Despite the needed increase in comprehensiveness of institutional statements of purpose noted above, such statements at most institutions visited by the authors currently remain focused solely upon the instructional, research, and public service aspects of the institution. Failure to include administrative and educational support activities in the Expanded Statement of Institutional Purpose over looks the contributions of major components of the institution and makes more difficult the task of the majority of the institution's employees (the staff) to demonstrate where their efforts support the accomplishment of the statement of purpose for the institution. In many of these cases, the connection of the AES units to the support of the institutional statement of purpose can be no more direct than to "create an environment" in which the primary purposes of the institution (instruction, research, and public service) can take place. This type of linkage is sufficient, but not as desirable as a clear and direct connection to the Expanded Statement of Institutional Purpose.

The need to establish "institutional effectiveness" involved in virtually all regional accrediting association requirements stipulates that AES units be able to show their support of the statement of purpose. This has led to progressively more institutions improving their Expanded Statement of Purpose to include in their institutional goals several statements which are specifically related to the work done by various administrative and educational support units on the campus. These statements serve as the "hooks" to which AES units can connect their contributions to the Expanded Statement of Institutional Purpose. Examples of such goal statements are shown below:

- To assist students in achieving their educational goals by making available quality student and educational support services.
- To improve educational support services (library, computer networking, database availability, instructional support, etc.) to increase access to information and communication on the campus.
- To continue to develop leadership and to instill in its students a sense of justice, moral courage, and tolerance for the views of others.
- To maintain efficient and effective administrative services to support the institution's instruction, research, and public service programs.
- To increase efforts to secure support from federal, state, and private sources.

As the assessment implementation process begins in an institution's administrative and educational units, the first step is a careful review of the existing statement of purpose for the institution. This review should determine whether AES units are going to need to be satisfied with "creating an environment" through which the statement of purpose can be achieved, or if there are specific goals within the Expanded Statement of Institutional Purpose which AES units need to address or support. Once this review is accomplished, AES units can turn to establishment of their own Unit Mission Statements.

Step One: An Approach That Works

One effective way of beginning the linkage process is for the administrative and educational support (AES) unit director to determine where the unit supports the expanded statement of institutional purpose. The director should take a highlighter and underline portions of the institution's mission and institutional goals that the unit supports. The mission and institutional goals statements are usually found in the first several pages of the institution's catalog.

STEP TWO—PREPARE THE ADMINISTRATIVE UNIT MISSION STATEMENT

At most campuses, for either external or internal reporting, administrative and educational support units have formulated a Unit Mission Statement. Some regional accrediting agencies (notably the Commission on Colleges, Southern Association of Colleges and Schools) require establishment of such a Unit Mission Statement for each administrative and educational support unit. The purpose of the Unit Mission Statement is to serve as the intermediary linkage between the institutional level Expanded Statement of Institutional Purpose and the more specific administrative objectives to be established by each administrative and educational support unit.

The Unit Mission Statement should:

- Describe the purpose of the unit—This should include areas of service responsibility and clients served
- Be relatively brief in length—A paragraph to two-thirds page, maximum
- Provide linkage to and support of the Expanded Statement of Institutional Purpose—As well as providing the linkage for statements of administrative objectives by the AES unit
- Be known by the employees within the unit who participated in its formulation

The Unit Mission Statement should highlight the major functions of the unit and, where appropriate, describe services or functions provided as well as key procedures conducted by personnel employed therein. Three examples of Unit Mission Statements concerning the Career Center, Accounting Office and the Library, are shown in Figure 7.

The relationship between the Unit Mission Statement and the Expanded Statement of Institutional Purpose constitutes Column "1" of the Five-Column Model previously illustrated in Figure 4 (page 30). Column "1" of the Office of the Registrar example shown in Figure 4, as well as several other examples, including that for the Career Center, Accounting Office and Library are shown in Figures 8-11 on the following pages.

The Unit Mission Statement is the key linkage both upward to the Expanded Statement of Institutional Purpose and to the more specific administrative objectives

Figure 7

Example Administrative and Educational Support Unit Mission Statements

Example Career Center Mission Statement

The mission of the career center is to aid students in the successful transition from academia to the world of work, by preparing students realistically for the world after graduation. To accomplish this goal, the Career Center offers an array of services from freshman year through graduation.

> Career Counseling and a variety of programs to assess skills, values and interests, three graded academic, elective 3-hour credit classes:
> Career Decision Making for freshman and sophomore level students
> Career and Life Planning for junior and senior level students
> Career Leadership Class for developing peer counselors who will present career information

A Career Information Center with both technological and traditional "paper" methods of self-exploration, occupational information, and exploration of the full range of employment opportunities and/or graduate studies, workshops, seminars and personal assistance in developing resumes, interview techniques and job search strategies is maintained. Opportunities for part-time and summer jobs, internships and full-time jobs upon graduation are publicized.

The Center's services and programs are designed to complement and enhance the academic mission of the university. Students who have made informed career decisions are motivated toward a career goal to obtain greater benefits from their marketability to employers upon graduation. Finally, graduates who are well prepared for the transition from education to the work environment will have greater choices of further opportunities.

Example Library Mission Statement

The university educates students to assume leadership roles in the state, nation, and world through its nationally recognized programs of undergraduate, graduate, and professional study. Its fundamental purpose is the creation and dissemination of knowledge. The university libraries support this mission. Specifically, the university libraries strive to meet the information needs of the academy, its students, faculty and staff, by employing contemporary knowledge management techniques to develop collections, provide access to information sources, and instruct individuals in contemporary bibliographic methodologies.

Example Accounting Office Mission Statement

The Accounting Office seeks (1) to provide administrators with accurate and timely financial data to assist them in the management of the institution's resources, and (2) to ensure that financial records are maintained in accordance with generally accepted accounting principles and guidelines as established by State and Federal agencies.

Figure 8

Office of the Registrar
One-Column Model

Institutional Mission/Goals Reference

To assist students in achieving their goals by making available quality student and educational support services.

Unit Mission Statement

The Registrar's Office is responsible for processing applications for admission, processing and reporting student enrollment, maintaining registered student records, receiving grades, and the processing of transcript information.

Figure 9

Career Center
One-Column Model

Institutional Mission/Goals Reference

(Goal 6) ….The University will continue to develop leadership and to instill in its students a sense of justice, moral courage, and tolerance for the views of others…improve admissions, academic, *career and placement counseling.*

Unit Mission Statement

… to assist students in transition from academia to the world of work by preparing students for life after graduation….the Career Center offers services which include: career counseling; 3 classes for academic credit, workshops and seminars on career-related subjects; assistance with resume writing and interviewing; and opportunities for part-time jobs, internships, and full-time jobs.

Figure 10

Accounting Office
One-Column Model

Institutional Mission/Goals Reference

Goal 7....The university will maintain efficient and effective administrative services to support the university's instructional, research, and public service programs.

Unit Mission Statement

The Accounting Office seeks (1) to provide administrators with accurate and timely financial data to assist them in the management of the institution's resources, and (2) to ensure that financial records are maintained in accordance with generally accepted accounting principles and guidelines as established by State and Federal agencies.

Figure 11

Library
One-Column Model

Institutional Mission/Goals Reference

Goal 4...To assist students in achieving their educational goals by making available quality student and educational support services.

Unit Mission Statement

....to support and stimulate teaching and learning by providing an environment in which instruction and research can flourish. The University Library aims to acquire, preserve, provide access to, and disseminate recorded knowledge in all its forms. Access will be provided through traditional and technological methods. The library will provide bibliographic, reference, and instructional support to student, faculty, staff and the community.

set by the unit (see Figure 12). Linkage to the institutional level is required by regional accrediting associations and essential in order to demonstrate institutional effectiveness.

Figure 12

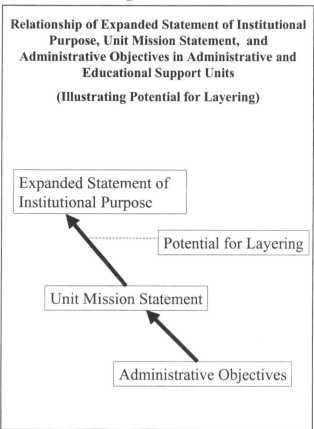

Relationship of Expanded Statement of Institutional Purpose, Unit Mission Statement, and Administrative Objectives in Administrative and Educational Support Units

(Illustrating Potential for Layering)

Expanded Statement of Institutional Purpose

Potential for Layering

Unit Mission Statement

Administrative Objectives

At institutions with smaller administrative or educational support structures, a mission statement prepared for the division (student services, financial affairs, advancement, etc.) may serve the purpose of the individual AES Unit Mission Statement. At larger institutions, the use of divisional mission statements becomes more questionable. Institutions should resist any more "layering" of mission statements (see Figure 12) than is absolutely necessary in order to keep the overall assessment process as simple and straightforward as possible. Layering takes place when administrators at various levels (vice president, associate vice president, executive director, etc.) establish another "layer" of objectives or mission statements which the subordinate units must either include or adopt in their establishment of administrative objectives. Excessive "layering" robs individual AES units of their autonomy, thereby substantially lessening the interest of AES staff in pursuing someone else's objectives. At large institutions which have distinctly separate AES support departments (units), it is recommended that each of these unit's mission statements link directly to the Expanded Statement of Institutional Purpose, rather than through a divisional (student life, administrative affairs, etc.) mission statement in order to keep linkages as uncomplicated as possible and to provide maximum opportunity for creativity and ownership by AES unit staff. Hence, the role of leadership at the divisional or vice presidential level becomes one of influencing their units' mission statements to ensure that desired service improvements are taking place.

Formulating the Unit Mission Statement

In large to medium size AES units, there are several ways through which to formulate the Unit Mission Statement. Perhaps the most effective is for the unit director to ask the individual staff personnel to list the services that they provide as well as those services provided by their co-workers. These listings should be disassociated from the individual employees submitting them to avoid "office politics," though often job descriptions provide valuable sources. The combined list of services to be discussed in the staff meeting provides a framework from which the Unit Mission Statement can emerge.

In preparing Unit Mission Statements for small or one-person offices, input from other sources will facilitate the statement's formulation. The solicitation of example Unit Mission Statements from AES units accomplishing similar functions at peer institutions can provide insight into one's own Unit Mission Statement. Another useful device is asking other administrators at your institution to identify the functions they believe your unit should or does perform. Both the opinions of your own campus colleagues as well as review of mission statements from your peers at other institutions may reveal surprising results.

The Unit Mission Statement should be reevaluated each year at the time of reformulating unit administrative objectives. Due to the nature of administrative and educational support units, it is not unusual for the AES Unit Mission Statement to need frequent revision. A number of factors, including individual personnel availability, staffing levels, and demands placed upon the unit by external agencies, may change unit functions and services from year to year. Once the draft statement is prepared/reviewed for currency, it should undergo a final editing and discussion among the staff prior to forwarding to the senior administrative officer (supervisor) to whom the unit reports.

The supervisor's review is essential to confirm that the key elements which the senior administrative officer seeks to accomplish are being addressed in the Unit Mission Statement. In practice, this often results in clarification of responsibilities which otherwise would have resulted in dysfunctional reporting relationship.

The first and second step in administrative assessment implementation are the conceptual cornerstone upon which the more specific portions of the unit assessment plan, and ultimately its assessment activities and use of results, are based. These two steps, "Establishing a Linkage to the Institution's Statement of Purpose" and "Preparing the Unit Mission Statement," are the foundation upon which all subsequent AES unit assessment activities are based. The unit administrative objectives, means of assessment, and criteria for success discussed in the balance of this chapter each ultimately relates to these initial two steps in the implementation process.

Step Two: An Approach That Works

Units often find themselves pressured to begin assessment activities as soon as possible. In such instances, AES unit heads can reduce the time required for writing the Unit Mission Statement by preparing a draft mission statement and then circulating it among AES unit staff and peers for additions and corrections. This process allows the Unit Mission Statement to be developed in a minimum amount of time while providing some AES unit staff input.

STEP THREE—FORMULATE ADMINISTRATIVE OBJECTIVES

Following the preparation of the AES Unit Mission Statement, it will be necessary to formulate specific administrative service objectives to implement the general concepts outlined in the Unit Mission Statement. These administrative objectives support the Unit Mission Statement and are the linkage to the means of assessment discussed in step four.

The bulk of AES units on a campus will identify administrative objectives, which will be "process oriented." These objectives describe how well the AES unit intends to function or improve its services. In administrative units, such as the Accounting Office, Bursar's Office, Physical Plant, Office of the Registrar, Public Relations, etc., administrative objectives which are "process oriented" are most common. Often these "process oriented" administrative objectives focus on specific functions or administrative procedures, which the unit personnel believe should be improved.

Educational support units such as the Library, Career Center, Counseling Center, Student Orientation, and other units that contribute directly to student learning often use a second type of administrative objective, one focused on the outcome of the student's involvement with the unit. These units can be expected to establish administrative objectives which are a mix of "process oriented" statements describing what the unit intends to accomplish and "outcomes oriented" administrative objectives describing what the clientele (students) will be able to accomplish following service by the unit. Not to have such a mix of statements in these areas is an unusual circumstance. These types of administrative objectives (as well as satisfaction oriented objectives) are described next.

Types of Administrative Objectives Common in AES Units

AES unit administrative objectives usually can be classified as process, outcome, or satisfaction oriented.

"Process oriented" statements of administrative objectives (as partially described earlier in this chapter) relate to what the AES unit intends to accomplish and are most frequently found to describe: a) the *level* or *volume* of unit activity, b) the *efficiency* with which the unit's processes are conducted, or c) *compliance* with external standards of "good practice in the field" or regulations.

Almost any AES unit on a campus can readily identify available measures of the volume of work, which it accomplishes. In the Office of the Registrar, this measure may be "number of students registered," while in the Bursar's Office it is "number of accounts maintained," or "transactions processed," or in the Center for Academic Advising, the "number of student contacts." It is not infrequent that AES units "justify their existence" based upon the amount of service provided or work accomplished and already keep extensive documentation regarding this matter.

Less frequently maintained by AES units are measures of "unit efficiency." Administrative objectives relating to such records of efficiency include measures of "cost per _____," or "number of _____ processed per full-time equivalent staff." These types of administrative objectives seek to analyze the unit's processes in terms of cost or efficiency compared to normative data at similar institutions. The NACUBO benchmarking project mentioned earlier and described later in this chapter is an excellent source of such normative comparisons.

Many "process oriented" statements of administrative objectives are taken from external statements of "good practice in the field." These types of external standards are either voluntarily adopted by the institution or are forced upon the unit by a regulatory body. Typically among those standards voluntarily adopted by a unit are those set forth by the Council for the Advancement of Standards (CAS) for the student affairs aspects of an institution. Areas in which CAS standards exist are shown in Figure 13. These standards are recognized throughout the student services field as representing what "should take place" in student affairs/services components at institutions of higher education.

In many cases, AES units at an institution are "bound" by regulatory requirements imposed by external agencies, hence, meeting these requirements often becomes an AES unit administrative objective. Exemplary of the influence of such external requirements are the American Institute of Certified Public Accountants (AICPA) standards on the accounting office at an institution, health department requirements on the institution's food service operations, and the fire marshal's standards on the institution's student housing operations and instructional laboratories.

Less common than "process oriented" administrative objectives, but equally acceptable are those "outcome oriented" administrative objectives concerning the ability of clients after services have been provided by the AES unit. Examples of this type of objective are: a) the ability of students or other clients to utilize library resources following an orientation to those services, b) the student's ability to prepare a resume based upon guidance provided in the Career Center, and c) the faculty's ability to utilize instructional media based upon equipment and training provided by the Media Resource Center.

Finally, client "satisfaction oriented" administrative objectives are the most common type of administrative objectives. These range from overall "client satisfaction" administrative objectives such as those frequently included on institutional graduating student or alumni surveys to more specific surveys of client satisfaction with

Figure 13

```
┌─────────────────────────────────────────────┐
│    Council For The Advancement Of Standards   │
│              Functional Area                  │
│          Standards And Guidelines             │
│                                               │
│     1.  Academic Advising                     │
│     2.  Admission Programs & Services         │
│     3.  Alcohol & Other Drug Programs         │
│     4.  Campus Activities                     │
│     5.  Career Planning & Placement           │
│     6.  College Unions                        │
│     7.  Commuter Student Programs             │
│     8.  Counseling Services                   │
│     9.  Disability Support Services           │
│    10.  Financial Aid                         │
│    11.  Fraternity & Sorority Advising        │
│    12.  Housing & Residential Life Programs   │
│    13.  International Student Programs & Services│
│    14.  Judicial Programs & Services          │
│    15.  Learning Assistance Programs          │
│    16.  Minority Student Programs & Services  │
│    17.  Outcome Assessment & Program Evaluation│
│    18.  Recreational Sports                   │
│    19.  Registrar Programs & Services         │
│    20.  Religious Programs                    │
│    21.  Student Leadership Programs           │
│    22.  Student Orientation Programs          │
│    23.  Women Student Programs & Services     │
└─────────────────────────────────────────────┘
```

components of individual services. Examples of each type of administrative objective are provided in Figure 14.

It is not uncommon to find process, outcomes, and client satisfaction oriented administrative objectives in a single AES unit's assessment plan. However, there is no requirement that any particular mix of these types of administrative objectives be utilized within an AES unit. It is important to understand that the means of assessment ultimately selected by the unit will measure the volume or efficiency of the *processes* conducted by the unit, the *ability* of the client after receipt of services, or the client's *satisfaction* following receipt of service. This means of assessment chosen will be directly and strongly impacted by the nature of the administrative objectives chosen. That is the reason that selection of the administrative objectives before identification of means of assessment is so important.

Figure 14

Examples: Statements of Intended Administrative and Educational Support Objectives

Outcome Statements:
1. Students will learn how to use library resources.
2. Graduates will have the ability to write a resume.

Process Statements:
1. Library will be efficient in book acquisitions.
2. The number of workshops provided by the Career Center will increase.
3. Accounting Office will promptly process vendor statements.

Satisfaction Statements:
1. Students will be satisfied with Library circulation service.
2. Vendors will report prompt payment.

Senior Administrative Officers' Preparation of Statements of Administrative Objectives

Supervisory, vice presidential level or deans' offices, that function primarily *to manage the services of others*, normally do not need to complete statements of administrative objectives. The effectiveness of these offices is measured through other means including the accomplishments of units reporting to them. However, in some instances a supervisory office also provides services. For example, an academic dean's office which a) provides academic advising services for the students within the college, school, or division; b) performs degree program completion audits for students prior to graduation and; c) houses the secretarial pool for the faculty of the college, school, or division. It would be entirely appropriate to establish a series of administrative objectives focusing on the services provided.

The Duration of Administrative Objectives

Normally, administrative objectives should be established for a period of roughly one year, which in many cases follows the institutional fiscal year or academic calendar year. In other instances, the time period may be lengthened to reflect accomplishments requiring a longer time. In this case, annual administrative objectives, ultimately building to the overall administrative objective are established. In other cases, administrative objectives may be as little as one semester or perhaps even less in duration. These instances most often take place regarding processes which themselves are short term in duration, such as reviews of institutional investment portfolios.

Since most administrative objectives are one-year or less in duration, this conveniently differentiates them from "strategic action plans" which are usually multi-year and focus on broad changes in unit processes.

Guidelines to Be Followed in Formulating Unit Administrative Objectives

When formulating administrative objectives, the following four principles or guidelines should be observed. Administrative objectives should be: (a) linked to the Unit Mission Statement (and hence to the Expanded Statement of Institutional Purpose), (b) realistic, (c) limited in number, and (d) measurable.

The administrative objectives established by a unit should link to and directly support the Unit Mission Statement. This linkage is reflected in the "Two-Column Models" shown in Figures 15-18 and is essential for turning what otherwise would be *unit* effectiveness into overall *institutional* effectiveness.

The statements of administrative objectives should be realistic in terms of the resources and support currently available within the unit. In many cases, AES units are tempted to use administrative objectives which may be related to their strategic action. These objectives often include some type of planning activity which needs to take place prior to providing the service. These planning objectives often represent an idealized set of objectives accomplishable only with substantial increases in resources or support provided to the unit. Such unrealistic objectives are seldom useful in the improvement of services provided by the unit and serve primarily to frustrate unit staff when resources or support are not available and, therefore, the objective is not achievable.

Overly modest and hence, unrealistic in terms of what the AES unit can actually accomplish, administrative objectives are often found in instances wherein the unit staff feels threatened. This often is observed at institutions that have (intentionally or inadvertently) tied assessment for *service improvement* to one type or another of administrative evaluation for *personnel decisions* (promotions, salary increases, etc.). This tendency is particularly strong in cases in which the institution has procrastinated in implementation to the point that it is attempting to find something already taking place to use for assessment of AES units, or in a circumstance in which there is an externally mandated process. Unit heads, in conjunction with their staff, need to identify administrative objectives for the unit which (within existing resources and personnel) stretch the unit's ability to the maximum in providing services for its clientele. This "stretching" needs to be done in an environment in which unit administrators are free to attempt these service improvements without the necessary fear that, if unsuccessful in improving services to the extent intended, the unit (or the administrators themselves) will be held accountable.

Figure 15

Office of the Registrar
Two-Column Model

Institutional Mission/Goal Reference

Goal #4: To assist students in achieving their educational goals by making available quality student and educational support services.

Unit Mission Statement

The Registrar's Office is responsible for processing applications for admission, processing and reporting student enrollment, maintaining registered student records, receiving grades, and the processing of transcript information.

Administrative Objectives

1. Increase student satisfaction with the overall registration process.

2. Shorten response time for transcript requests.

3. Provide accurate class enrollment data.

Figure 16

Career Center
Two-Column Model

Institutional Mission/Goal Reference

(Goal 6) ...The University will continue to develop leadership and to instill in its students a sense of justice, moral courage, and tolerance for the views of others...improve admissions, academic, *career and placement counseling.*

Unit Mission Statement

... to assist students in transition from academia to the world of work by preparing students for life after graduation....the Career Center offers services which include: career counseling; 3 classes for academic credit, workshops and seminars on career-related subjects; assistance with resume writing and interviewing; and opportunities for part-time jobs, internships, and full-time jobs.

Administrative Objectives

1. Graduates will be satisfied with services provided by the Career Center.

2. Students will be aware of employment opportunities.

3. The number of opportunities for students to find employment will increase.

Figure 17

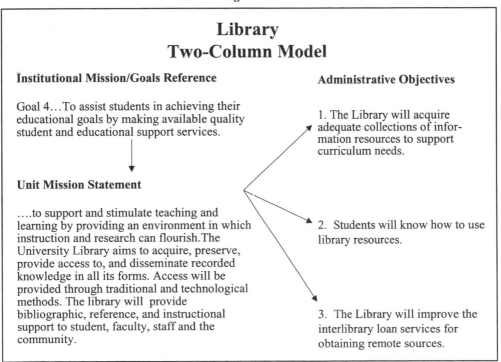

Accounting Office
Two-Column Model

Institutional Mission/Goals Reference

Goal 7.... the university will maintain efficient and effective administrative services to support the university's instructional, research, and public service programs.

Unit Mission Statement

The Accounting Office seeks (1) to provide administrators with accurate and timely financial data to assist them in the management of the institution's resources, and (2) to ensure that financial records are maintained in accordance with generally accepted accounting principles and guidelines as established by State and Federal agencies.

Administrative Objectives

1. Maintain financial systems in accordance with commonly accepted accounting practices.

2. Provide monthly financial reports by object of expenditure concerning expenditures and remaining balances to departments.

3. Process vendor statements for services promptly.

Figure 18

Library
Two-Column Model

Institutional Mission/Goals Reference

Goal 4...To assist students in achieving their educational goals by making available quality student and educational support services.

Unit Mission Statement

....to support and stimulate teaching and learning by providing an environment in which instruction and research can flourish.The University Library aims to acquire, preserve, provide access to, and disseminate recorded knowledge in all its forms. Access will be provided through traditional and technological methods. The library will provide bibliographic, reference, and instructional support to student, faculty, staff and the community.

Administrative Objectives

1. The Library will acquire adequate collections of information resources to support curriculum needs.

2. Students will know how to use library resources.

3. The Library will improve the interlibrary loan services for obtaining remote sources.

Often AES units identify during the first iteration of this process only those administrative objectives which they are certain the unit can accomplish. They want to test the assessment procedure until they have evidence that the process is being used for improvement, rather than personnel accountability. In the second iteration of the process, the same AES unit (having seen that the process was not punitive, but supportive) frequently identifies much more ambitious administrative objectives reflective of its desire to improve AES unit operations, performance, and service.

Perhaps the most common mistake made in implementation of institutional effectiveness and assessment activities is the attempt to assess everything all the time. This frequently results in an extensive list of administrative objectives and the necessary means of assessment to evaluate the accomplishment of each. Unless restrained, the amount of assessment effort required to assess (conduct, analyze, and document) the administrative objectives identified becomes so burdensome that little or no assessment can actually take place. Participants then become frustrated and the process never leads to the improvement of services intended. Unless the number of administrative objectives subject to assessment at any one time is limited, any AES unit will "choke and die" on the assessment activities required.

An administrative and educational support unit should first identify a potential long list of administrative objectives supporting the activities described in the Unit Mission Statement (see Figure 19, Short List/Long List Concept). From this long list, the unit should choose *between three and five administrative objectives for assessment at any one time*. Those administrative objectives selected initially should be:

- Targeted on those areas which the unit staff believe can be improved by using the currently available resources and personnel
- Related to the services the unit provides
- Relatively easy to assess within one assessment cycle
- Directly under control of the AES unit

Do not do away with the "Long List" of potential administrative objectives. After one or more assessment cycles, evidence will be forthcoming indicating which of the initial three to five statements of administrative objectives are being accomplished or have reached a plateau based upon the personnel and resources available, and the unit will want to reevaluate the long list. As an example, students' rating of food services on most campuses will never meet the top level of satisfaction and probably plateau (no matter what changes are made) because traditionally students prefer their mom's home cooking. Whenever existing administrative objectives are clearly being met to the maximum extent feasible, the unit should select another administrative objective after review of the Long List from the previous year and any new objectives that have been added.

Annually, AES units should pause to review their accomplishment of administrative objectives and have the opportunity for important discussions concerning continuance of these administrative objectives or selection of new objectives, either

Figure 19

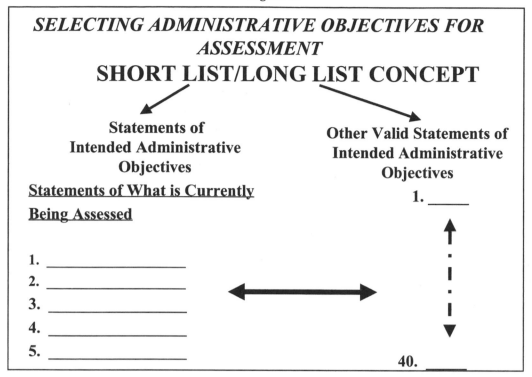

from the Long List or based upon other factors. Due to the service nature of AES units, their administrative objectives change more frequently than those of educational programs. Frequently, new administrative objectives are formulated based upon the "use of results" of the previous year's administrative objectives. Thus, a dynamic process —in which staff periodically review (a) that which they are attempting to accomplish (administrative objectives), (b) the means for measuring their accomplishment, and (c) subsequent use of results to improve service—is built into the fabric of the AES unit's yearly activities and demonstrates a systematic process of improvement in services.

Finally, virtually all statements of administrative objectives are subject to relatively direct quantitative measurement regarding their accomplishment. Particularly in the areas related to student development, measurement can be a complex process. In many cases, administrative objectives established in the student development area will relate to the acquisition by the student of a set of values, moral principles, or certain personal attributes. Under these circumstances, direct questioning of clients regarding their acquisition of the values identified often yields only the "socially acceptable response" and provides little useful assessment information. In these cases, student development staff will need to identify client actions reflective of acquisition of the values identified. This may result in indirect measures of student acquisition of the values identified. The Office of Student Life may choose as one of its administrative objectives:

"Students will make a personal commitment to the responsibilities of citizenship," as measured by participation in student elections. The Office of the Chaplain may choose as its administrative objective: "Students will demonstrate a commitment to Judeo-Christian beliefs."

AES units need to be careful in *selecting* their administrative objectives from the Long List to ensure that each *selected* objective includes only one concept or service for assessment. In many cases, units, in seeking to be all inclusive, combine a number of potential administrative objectives from the Long List into a single compound administrative objective for the Short List. This is frequently the case when administrative objectives on the Short List are found to contain commas, semicolons, or conjunctions. While succeeding in limiting the apparent number of administrative objectives, this combining of previously separate administrative objectives leads to exceedingly complex objectives with multiple means of assessment necessary for each. To accomplish this much assessment requires many more staff hours than most AES units have to give, leads to a reduction of service to clientele, and causes a good deal of frustration on the part of the staff.

In summary, administrative objectives should be clearly linked to a Unit Mission Statement targeted on service improvement, realistic in terms of current resources and services, limited in number to between three and five for assessment at any one time, within the control of the unit, and measurable through the means of assessment described in Step 4.

The Need to Review and Change Administrative Objectives

There are two ways to "win" and two ways to "lose" in demonstrating a unit's effectiveness. The *first* win is to accomplish the unit's administrative objectives. This clearly is a time for celebration. The *second* win is to not be accomplishing the unit's administrative objectives (based on the assessment data gathered), but making improvements in service based upon use of results of assessment. This win comes from using the results to put a "fix" in place to better reach the desired service improvement. Either demonstration is clearly a win in assessment circles. Making changes based on assessment results demonstrates the genuineness of the institution's commitment to self-improvement. Prolonged measurement of administrative objectives previously accomplished casts doubt on the sincerity with which the unit is actually attempting to improve its services.

The two ways to lose regarding assessment activities are also frequently encountered on campuses. The *first* of these is simply for administrative and educational support units not to do assessment for the improvement of services. There is no reason at this stage of the assessment movement that this circumstance should be encountered; however, it still exists on too many campuses. This is most often the result of ignorance of the process, rather than willful intention to defy. The *second* way to lose is to have substantive assessment information (such as institutional level client satisfaction measures) readily available on the campus without use being made of this information to improve services. On numerous campuses, the results of graduating student, alumni, and other surveys and questionnaires providing potentially very useful assessment information are simply not communicated to the AES units involved or the use of this information for service improvement is not part of the unit's activities.

Step Three: An Approach That Works

Assuming that the unit has developed a Unit Mission Statement, formulating administrative objectives by involving the professional staff can be accomplished in four hours or less. First, the AES unit head should schedule two staff meetings. One meeting should be on Friday afternoon, the last two hours of the working day. The other should be on the following Monday, the last two hours of the working day.

Prior to the first meeting, have all staff anonymously submit to the unit head three suggestions of unit functions (refer to the unit's mission statement) that should be improved during the next assessment cycle. Explain that these improvements need to be based on the personnel and resources available to the unit. This forces even the most reluctant and shy staff member to become involved in the process. The AES unit head compiles the suggestions submitted into one list. Though they may be grouped by subject, be very careful to make sure all suggestions (soon to become objectives) are exactly as the staff worded them. Make copies of this list for all staff personnel. During the first staff meeting, discuss all the suggested potential administrative objectives (Long List) and clarify what is meant by each. Make clear to the staff that the charge is to select only three from this list. Spend most of this initial staff meeting time discussing and deciding which three suggestions or objectives should be assigned to the Short List. If objectives have previously been selected, it is not unusual during this first meeting for the staff to decide to remove one of the objectives on the Short List and replace it with one initially placed on the Long List.

Over the weekend, without being directed the staff will think about the objectives and therefore will be better prepared for the second staff meeting. The first hour of the second staff meeting is usually spent "wordsmithing" the objectives selected. However, it is not unusual for the staff to decide to eliminate one of the objectives and replace it with another objective still on the long list. The last hour of this staff meeting is spent on the selection of the means of assessment and the criteria for success. This activity will naturally lead staff to identification of the means for assessment of the accomplishment of these administrative objectives and then to their criteria for success.

STEP FOUR—IDENTIFY MEANS OF ASSESSMENT AND CRITERIA FOR SUCCESS

The first three steps in formulating the unit assessment plan ("Establishment of the Linkage to the Institutional Statement of Purpose," "Preparation of the Unit Mission Statement," as well as "Formulation of Administrative Objectives") are in many ways the necessary preliminaries before the "main event" in the creation of the AES unit assessment plan or three-column model, "Identification of Means of Assessment and the Criteria for Success."

In transition from administrative objectives to the identification of the specific means of assessment and criteria for success, previously acceptable generalities such as "efficiently," "effectively," "to their satisfaction," etc., must become operational to the point of measurement. It is in this process of identification of means of assessment that the "when," "how," and "how well," of assessment are addressed:

- "When" will assessment activities take place?
- Where will we find information that will reflect accomplishment of our objective?
- Exactly "How" will the assessment be accomplished?
- "How well" should the unit perform on the means of assessment identified, if the unit is functioning the way it should?

The means of assessment identified should flow from and remain directly related to the specific administrative objective which it is designed to measure. The tendency in some AES units is to first identify means of assessment and then "back into" administrative objectives. This is often seen as a "quick and dirty" means for completing an assessment plan based upon assessment activities that may already (often for other reasons) be in place. While such action does facilitate creation of the assessment plan, the assessment activities described often do not yield information which unit staff find useful for service improvement. Hence, the time saved in lack of creation of the plan is more than lost in the lack of useful information and the unit finds itself assessing those service areas which are functioning well instead of focusing on those areas where service improvement can occur.

A well-formulated administrative objective will automatically dictate the means of assessment to be used. When reading the administrative objective, the AES staff needs to constantly ask the questions, "How will we know if this is being accomplished?" and "What will provide us this information?" The answer to the question, "What will provide us this information?" leads the AES unit quickly to identify their means of assessment.

Retention of the relationship between each administrative objective and the specific means of assessment identified is also important in fostering use of results. In many instances, AES units lose track over time of the relationship (shown in the example "Three-Column Models" provided at the end of this chapter) between the administrative objectives and the specific means of assessment selected. When this takes place, it is also frequently found that the use of assessment results to improve services diminishes substantially.

The clear message in these paragraphs is that it pays substantial dividends to follow the four-step process suggested from establishment of the linkage to the institutional statement of purpose and Unit Mission Statement through formulation of administrative objectives and subsequently to the identification of means of assessment and criteria for success as described in the following pages. The alternative is to pay a steep price in wasted time, energy, and money.

All of the regional accrediting associations stress the importance of multiple means of assessment whenever possible. Assessment remains in its infancy as a field and it is important, wherever possible, that several means of assessment are utilized to ascertain the accomplishment of each administrative objective.

While the types of assessment utilized in educational support and administrative units is truly limited only by the imagination of the staff involved, most assessment activities can be categorized as client satisfaction measures, direct counts, results of external evaluation, and outcome measures. Each of these means of assessment has some specific characteristics, strengths and limitations which are discussed in the following paragraphs.

Attitudinal Assessment in Administrative and Educational Support Units

The most common type of assessment activities within administrative and educational support units is one version or another of client satisfaction measures. Where such measures are considered weak and an indirect means of assessment for instructional programs, they are often the only and/or best means for administrative and educational support units to assess the success of the services. Such measures are relatively common on campuses across the United States and can be valuable sources of information for improvement of administrative and educational support services.

The utilization of satisfaction measures requires the identification of the administrative or educational support unit's clients.For most educational support units on a campus, students constitute their primary service recipients. However, a unit's services may also be extended to other clientele. As an example, the Admissions Office provides information to both potential students and their *parents*. The Career Center provides services to both students and to *employers*. The office charged with the responsibility for coordination of cultural events provides services to students and often *members of the public* who also attend such performances. The library at most institutions, while primarily focused on service to students, certainly provides services to *faculty* and the *public*. Finally, some administrative units on campus provide services only indirectly related to current students. These include Media Services for *faculty*, Human Resources for *employees*, the Alumni Office for *former students* and Physical Plant for *institutional departments*. In any of these cases, an early determination of the specific clientele served by a unit is essential to the conduct of client satisfaction surveys.

Institutional level client satisfaction or attitudinal measures discussed are designed, produced and processed locally or conducted utilizing national standardized surveys. These two sources of institutional or general surveys (locally developed or standardized) have rather distinct advantages and disadvantages.

National standardized surveys have the advantages of ready availability and normative data for comparison purposes. American Colleges Testing (ACT), Educational Testing Service (ETS), and The College Board in conjunction with the National Center for Higher Education Management Systems, and Noel Levitz all vend excellent surveys, which include opportunities for client satisfaction feedback regarding administrative and educational support services.

Each of these vendors will provide, on very short notice, well designed instruments, suggestions for their distribution and in many cases standardized reports of client satisfaction with AES unit services. For an additional cost, most of these firms will also, (a) provide custom processing of the results as dictated by the institution and/or, (b) actually process, mail and distribute the results of the survey to campus AES units. Each of the instruments provided by the vendors referenced also allow the institution to compare client satisfaction with unit services to that in similar units at other institutions.

Particularly in highly competitive service areas such as Admissions, Financial Aid, Student Orientation, etc., it is important for an institution to know how their unit's services compare to competitors' level of services. In still other areas such as parking, food services, financial aid, and campus security, the question is not "Are clients satisfied with services?" The question is "Are students more dissatisfied with services at our institution than at comparable institutions?" Only normative data provided by national standardized client satisfaction surveys can provide the institution with (a) information concerning its services compared with direct competitors and (b) reasonable levels of satisfaction with areas that are traditionally less well thought of by clients.

On the other hand, nationally standardized surveys exhibit some clear limitations. Because administrative and educational support structures are not identical from campus to campus, these surveys must utilize generic descriptions of AES units to which clients are asked to relate their satisfaction. In most cases, this generic unit title is appropriate, however, in some instances there isn't a clear relationship between the title of the AES unit on the standardized questionnaire and the campus identity of the particular service unit. These general descriptions often do not work well for service areas that are part of an "umbrella unit." An example of this type of problem is a client's response regarding satisfaction with library services on a campus having three undergraduate and two graduate libraries. Additionally, a client's response to satisfaction with food services may refer to those offered by the institution in the dining hall, fast food outlets operating in the student center, or the fraternity/sorority house dining rooms.

In addition to this problem with unit identification, standardized client satisfaction surveys frequently do not cover some of the more unique services such as student pharmacy, transportation services, and museums found on some campuses. These unique services are quite often very important to the institution, form part of their character, and will need to be included in either the additional items which an institution can add to these standardized surveys or on a second survey.

Nationally standardized surveys or questionnaires are also more expensive in terms of out-of-pocket cost than locally developed instruments. Their cost ranges from several dollars per instrument to much more based upon the number of surveys, specific services required by the campus, and other factors.

The institution also needs to be careful about the peer group with whom their client satisfaction information is compared. It would be inappropriate to compare client satisfaction measures relating to admissions services of relatively small private residential institutions with those of urban institutions enrolling large numbers of part-time evening students. The services offered are simply not comparable and such comparison would do both types of institutions an injustice. Fortunately, the vendors referenced allow institutions to identify peer groups of institutions exhibiting similar characteristics. However, the institution needs to request such a peer group comparison, rather than accepting the national normative group. The additional cost for such service is more than warranted in the improved information available

Finally, standardized institutional level surveys generally lack institutional identification in their appearance. These instruments appear to be from a specific *vendor* rather than from the institution to whom the respondent will have naturally much greater allegiance. Those institutions selecting to utilize national standardized surveys that are distributed by mail should ensure that they are forwarded with a cover letter on distinctive stationery from the chief executive officer of the institution.

Who chooses to utilize nationally standardized survey instruments? These nationally standardized survey instruments are most frequently chosen by relatively smaller institutions who lack the necessary staff support services (usually institutional research components) to construct their own instrumentation. They are also chosen by institutions feeling a particularly urgent need to "get some assessment data." Such institutions can move from this realization to the receipt of nationally standardized survey results within a matter of months, though at a considerable price.

A brief description of each of the attitudinal assessment instruments referenced in this section is contained in Appendix B of this publication. Information concerning the national contact through which to get additional material regarding each instrument is also provided.

The alternative to use of nationally standardized surveys for assessment of client satisfaction is the local production of surveys by the institution. This choice is more commonly exercised at larger institutions employing staff sufficient to produce quality survey instruments. Locally developed instrumentation represents the institution and should convey an image of professionalism. Unfortunately, this is not always found to be the case in locally produced surveys.

Locally developed measures of client satisfaction have a number of advantages. First, the items concerning client satisfaction can be tailored exactly to institutional specific services, structures, and titles. Thus, there is no doubt that the results of the survey link directly to the individual AES units. While not apparent to the respondent, items included can utilize the exact wording found in the AES unit's administrative objectives. A second advantage of locally developed measures is the ability to adjust or change survey items, occasionally allowing the unit to alter the focus of its client satisfaction responses as its administrative objectives change. The items on a locally developed satisfaction survey can be weighted in number to seek more specific information about particular service areas of institutional interest. As an example, if the institution believes that it can improve student housing, the number of questions relating to that subject can be easily expanded on short notice with locally developed surveys. Finally, the questionnaires or surveys themselves can be attractively printed and of public relations or identity value to the institution. An example of such is shown in Figure 20, which is printed in red and blue (the school colors) with the CEO's signature.

The most obvious disadvantage of locally developed surveys of client satisfaction relates to comparability of results. First, unlike standardized surveys, there are no normative data for the comparison of underappreciated services such as parking, food services, etc. Second, it is not possible to directly compare client satisfaction with peer or competitive groups or institutions, although the authors have noted not terribly surprising similarities between some locally developed survey items and those included on nationally standardized surveys. Some institutions utilizing this approach have also, through one means or another, obtained national normative data against which to compare their own locally developed results. However, even this comparison does not provide the direct peer group comparison possible through the vendors noted.

The single greatest disadvantage to locally developed client satisfaction measures is their relative labor intensiveness and the amount of time necessary to prepare quality surveys at most institutions. Most locally developed client satisfaction surveys take between six months and a year to design, layout, distribute, and prepare the programming necessary for report processing. This effort can easily occupy the time of one staff member for this period and for the institution seeking to move quickly to acquire assessment data, this is not a viable course of action. On the other hand, once these instruments are designed and ready for processing, the out-of-pocket or per unit cost and the time needed for conducting such locally developed surveys diminishes substantially.

During the last ten years, great strides have been made in easing the design of locally developed questionnaires. Software from vendors such as Bubble Publishing, National Computer Systems, and Scantron has been developed which combines into a single software package the ability to design, process, and tabulate results of locally developed questionnaires. This software, coupled with the development of slow-speed optical character readers, enable an institution to establish a facility for designing very attractive and creditable questionnaires, processing them and providing useful information to users for under $10,000. A brief description of some of the packages provided by these vendors and the address through which they may be contacted is shown in Appendix C.

The choice of locally developed or standardized instrumentation is certainly one which is unique to each institution. Either type of approach will provide quality information that may be utilized to improve services.

Figure 20

Mark Reflex® by NCS EM-161209-2:654321   ED06   Printed in U.S.A.

THE UNIVERSITY OF MISSISSIPPI
GRADUATING STUDENT SURVEY

OFFICE USE ONLY

CONGRATULATIONS UPON COMPLETION OF YOUR DEGREE REQUIREMENTS AT OLE MISS! As an alumna or alumnus of our institution, I know that you take pride in your accomplishment and want to help further improve the educational experiences enjoyed by those who follow you at Ole Miss. To gather information concerning your Ole Miss experience, this brief questionnaire is provided for your completion. It asks for information about yourself and your plans after graduation, as well as the extent to which you are satisfied with Ole Miss in general, University services, and your specific degree program. Your answers will remain confidential and will be used to improve your alma mater's academic programs and administrative services. Please return this questionnaire when you file your Application for Diploma in the Office of the Registrar.

Robert C. Khayat, Chancellor

DEGREE PROGRAM CODE

USE NO. 2 PENCIL ONLY

CORRECT MARK ○ ● ○   INCORRECT MARKS ⦸ ⊘ ⊗

BIOGRAPHICAL/ENROLLMENT DATA Indicate only one response for each item by marking the appropriate circle.

1. GENDER
○ Male
○ Female

2. RACE
○ White
○ Black
○ Other

3. CITIZENSHIP
○ U.S.
○ Other

4. RESIDENCY AT TIME OF ADMISSION
○ Resident of Mississippi
○ Non-resident of Mississippi

5. CURRENT AGE
○ 22 or under
○ 23–25
○ 26–28
○ 29–31
○ 32–34
○ 35 or older

6. CURRENT STATUS
○ Undergraduate
○ Graduate

7A. (UNDERGRADUATE STUDENTS ONLY) WHILE PURSUING THIS DEGREE, DID YOU:
○ Originally enroll (and remain) at Ole Miss
○ Transfer from a 2-year institution
○ Transfer from a 4-year institution

11. ARE YOU ACTIVE IN AN OLE MISS SOCIAL FRATERNITY OR SORORITY?
○ Yes
○ No

7B. (GRADUATE & LAW STUDENTS ONLY) UNDERGRADUATE DEGREE FROM:
○ Ole Miss
○ Other institution

8. NUMBER OF YEARS IN ATTENDANCE AT OLE MISS
○ One   ○ Four
○ Two   ○ Five
○ Three ○ Six+

9. PLEASE ESTIMATE YOUR CUMULATIVE GPA (including only Ole Miss courses) UPON COMPLETION OF THIS DEGREE.
○ 3.75+   ○ 2.50–2.74
○ 3.50–3.74 ○ 2.25–2.49
○ 3.25–3.49 ○ 2.00–2.24
○ 3.00–3.24 ○ Below 2.00
○ 2.75–2.99

10. NUMBER OF SEMESTERS YOU HAVE LIVED IN AN OLE MISS RESIDENCE HALL
○ None   ○ Three
○ One   ○ Four
○ Two   ○ Five+

12. AVERAGE NUMBER OF HOURS EMPLOYED (ON/OFF CAMPUS) PER WEEK DURING THE PAST YEAR
○ None ○ 1–10 ○ 11–20 ○ 21–30 ○ 31–40 ○ 40+

PLANS FOLLOWING GRADUATION Indicate only one response for each item by marking the appropriate circle.

13. What are your immediate employment plans?
(a) I plan to continue working in the same job I had prior to completing this educational program.
(b) I plan to work in a job I recently obtained.
(c) I am currently looking for a job.
(d) I do not plan to work outside the home.
(e) I plan to continue my education before working.
(f) I have not yet formulated my employment plans.

14. If you indicated in #13 that you currently have or will be starting a new job, to what extent is it related to your major or area of study at Ole Miss?

Is the job in Mississippi?

(a) Directly related.
(b) Somewhat related.
(c) Not related.

(a) Yes.
(b) No.

15. Do you currently have plans for additional education?
(a) No, not at this time.
(b) Yes, I plan to reenroll at this institution.
(c) Yes, I plan to enroll at another institution. *
(d) Yes, I have been accepted for enrollment at another institution. *
(e) I am currently undecided about additional education.

*If you chose responses "c" or "d" above, please indicate name of institution you will attend. →

16. If you indicated in #15 that you plan to continue your education, what is the highest degree you plan to earn?
(a) Master's degree
(b) Specialist degree (e.g., Ed.S.)
(c) Professional degree (e.g., medicine, law, theology)
(d) Doctoral degree (e.g., Ph.D., Ed.D., D.B.A.)

GENERAL LEVEL OF SATISFACTION WITH ATTENDANCE AT THE UNIVERSITY (Undergraduate Students Only)

For each of the following items which apply, please indicate the extent of your agreement with the statement as it describes your experience at Ole Miss.

Within my degree program or because of my experiences at Ole Miss, I:	NOT APPLICABLE	STRONGLY AGREE	AGREE	NEUTRAL	DISAGREE	STRONGLY DISAGREE
17. Acquired a basic knowledge in the liberal arts (humanities, social sciences, and natural sciences).	NA	SA	A	N	D	SD
18. Felt academically challenged.	NA	SA	A	N	D	SD
19. Developed the ability to write effectively.	NA	SA	A	N	D	SD
20. Felt adequately prepared for graduate study in my major field.	NA	SA	A	N	D	SD
21. Was prepared to assume the responsibilities of my chosen profession.	NA	SA	A	N	D	SD
22. Developed the ability to express myself effectively through speaking.	NA	SA	A	N	D	SD
23. Developed multicultural and global perspectives.	NA	SA	A	N	D	SD
24. Would recommend to others that they study within the same program at Ole Miss.	NA	SA	A	N	D	SD
25. Would recommend Ole Miss to prospective students.	NA	SA	A	N	D	SD

Page Two
Continue Figure 20

OPINIONS CONCERNING UNIVERSITY ENVIRONMENT AND SERVICES (Graduate and Undergraduate Students)

Please indicate your level of satisfaction with each of the following University environmental conditions and services which you have used or directly experienced.

Environment and Services	NOT APPLICABLE OR DID NOT USE	VERY SATISFIED	SATISFIED	NEUTRAL	UN-SATISFIED	VERY UN-SATISFIED
26. Admissions	NA	VS	S	N	U	VU
27. Telephone Registration	NA	VS	S	N	U	VU
28. Regular Registration	NA	VS	S	N	U	VU
29. Fee Payment Process	NA	VS	S	N	U	VU
30. Bursar Office Services	NA	VS	S	N	U	VU
31. Academic Advising in School or College	NA	VS	S	N	U	VU
32. University Counseling Center	NA	VS	S	N	U	VU
33. Teaching and Learning Center Services/Disability Services	NA	VS	S	N	U	VU
34. Recognition and Promotion of Cultural Diversity	NA	VS	S	N	U	VU
35. Student Housing and Residence Life Services and Programs	NA	VS	S	N	U	VU
36. Student Programming Board Programs and Activities	NA	VS	S	N	U	VU
37. Department of Campus Recreation	NA	VS	S	N	U	VU
38. International Student Advisory Services	NA	VS	S	N	U	VU
39. Dean of Students Office	NA	VS	S	N	U	VU
40. Student Media/Newspaper, Yearbook, Radio, and Television	NA	VS	S	N	U	VU
41. Financial Aid Processed in Timely Manner	NA	VS	S	N	U	VU
42. University Police Department Public Safety Services	NA	VS	S	N	U	VU
43. Student Health Service	NA	VS	S	N	U	VU
44. Student Health Education Presentations/Programs/Counseling	NA	VS	S	N	U	VU
45. Student Health Center Pharmacy	NA	VS	S	N	U	VU
46. Career Services Center Information	NA	VS	S	N	U	VU
47. Financial Aid Services	NA	VS	S	N	U	VU
48. Food Services	NA	VS	S	N	U	VU
49. Overall Classroom Conditions	NA	VS	S	N	U	VU
50. Condition and Maintenance of University Grounds	NA	VS	S	N	U	VU
51. J.D. Williams Library and its Music and Science Branch Libraries	NA	VS	S	N	U	VU
52. Law Library	NA	VS	S	N	U	VU
53. Computer Center Services	NA	VS	S	N	U	VU
54. Bookstore	NA	VS	S	N	U	VU
55. Graduate School Office	NA	VS	S	N	U	VU

ITEMS RELATED TO YOUR DEGREE PROGRAM

While the opinions you expressed above concerning the University in general are important, your thoughts about your specific degree program are most important. When you received this form, you were also provided a separate sheet of colored paper with items (numbered 56–75) that relate directly to your degree program. Please indicate below the extent of your agreement with each statement contained on the colored paper.

	NOT APPLICABLE	STRONGLY AGREE	AGREE	NEUTRAL	DISAGREE	STRONGLY DISAGREE		NOT APPLICABLE	STRONGLY AGREE	AGREE	NEUTRAL	DISAGREE	STRONGLY DISAGREE
56.	NA	SA	A	N	D	SD	66.	NA	SA	A	N	D	SD
57.	NA	SA	A	N	D	SD	67.	NA	SA	A	N	D	SD
58.	NA	SA	A	N	D	SD	68.	NA	SA	A	N	D	SD
59.	NA	SA	A	N	D	SD	69.	NA	SA	A	N	D	SD
60.	NA	SA	A	N	D	SD	70.	NA	SA	A	N	D	SD
61.	NA	SA	A	N	D	SD	71.	NA	SA	A	N	D	SD
62.	NA	SA	A	N	D	SD	72.	NA	SA	A	N	D	SD
63.	NA	SA	A	N	D	SD	73.	NA	SA	A	N	D	SD
64.	NA	SA	A	N	D	SD	74.	NA	SA	A	N	D	SD
65.	NA	SA	A	N	D	SD	75.	NA	SA	A	N	D	SD

COMMENTS

Please feel free to add your written comments in the space provided at the right and return this form to the Office of the Registrar at the time you file your Application for Diploma.

Institutional Level Attitudinal Assessment in AES Units

At the *institutional level,* there are three primary constituencies or groups of clientele (enrolled and/or graduating students, alumni, and employees) that are frequently asked to complete surveys or questionnaires indicating their level of satisfaction with services provided by the institution's AES units. In each of these cases, an institution-wide survey is conducted with items specifically relating to satisfaction with varying AES services provided on campus.

Enrolled and/or graduating students are the most commonly surveyed constituency concerning their satisfaction with institutional AES services. Surveys of the institution's currently enrolled students enjoy the advantages of coverage of all student levels and thus, provide "early warning" of the disintegration of services provided to freshman and sophomore students. At the same time, the primary disadvantages of surveying only currently enrolled students are, (a) the responses by freshman and sophomore students offer only a limited exposure to institutional services and, (b) the mechanics of getting a representative or random sample *return* of the institutional level questionnaire may be challenging. On the other hand, polling students at the time of their graduation regarding satisfaction with institutional services has the distinct advantage of reflecting more depth and breadth of service experience (two, four, or more years). Surveys of currently enrolled students can provide equally useful information, though in the authors' opinion these types of results should be used to supplement and provide "early warning" of conditions ultimately confirmed by the graduating student survey. By the time students reach the point of graduation, they can express their satisfaction or lack thereof, with not one registration process, but between four and eight registration experiences. This depth of experience mitigates against the "one bad experience" with the service that sometimes overly influences the newer students' responses. Also, numerous institutional services such as Career Center activities are often not utilized until the end of the student's program and hence are not sufficiently covered in a survey of currently enrolled students. Additionally, inclusion of a graduating student survey in the "out-processing stream" at the time of the students' graduation can be accomplished and will assure a 95% plus response rate. The primary limitation of graduating student surveys relates to their delay in exposure of services that have deteriorated until the students' senior year. If services typically provided at the time of entry into the institution (admissions, new student orientation, counseling, explanation of library usage, intramural sports, etc.) deteriorate, it will probably be three to four years (at the end of entering students' degree programs) before student dissatisfaction with these services is reflected on graduating student surveys.

The best means through which to comprehensively gather student reaction to AES unit support services is a combination of graduating and enrolled student surveys. If it is not feasible for a campus to administer both, it is the authors' suggestion that a campus choose to implement a graduating student survey. A graduating student survey similar to that shown in Figure 20 should be implemented on a continuing (annual) basis at an institution. Such a survey will yield the most useful AES assessment information available. Graduating student surveys can be processed to

Figure 21

THE UNIVERSITY OF MISSISSIPPI
GRADUATING STUDENT SURVEY SUMMARY OF RESPONSES
FY 1998-1999, SUMMER 1999

	Not Applicable		Very Satisfied		Satisfied		Neutral		Unsatisfied		Very Unsat.		Ave.
ENVIRONMENT AND SERVICES													
54) BOOKSTORE	58	(2%)	355	(15%)	1,175	(49%)	379	(16%)	257	(11%)	152	(6%)	3.6
Sex: Male	21	(1%)	132	(6%)	497	(21%)	197	(8%)	132	(6%)	77	(3%)	3.5
Female	37	(2%)	221	(9%)	677	(29%)	181	(8%)	124	(5%)	75	(3%)	3.7
Race: White	48	(2%)	278	(12%)	960	(41%)	302	(13%)	197	(8%)	111	(5%)	3.6
Black	6	(0%)	56	(2%)	140	(6%)	32	(1%)	27	(1%)	19	(1%)	3.7
Other	3	(0%)	18	(1%)	70	(3%)	42	(2%)	28	(1%)	20	(1%)	3.2
Citizenship: U.S.	54	(2%)	341	(14%)	1,108	(47%)	327	(14%)	227	(10%)	131	(6%)	3.6
Other	3	(0%)	14	(1%)	62	(3%)	52	(2%)	29	(1%)	21	(1%)	3.1
Residency at Time of Admission													
MS	46	(2%)	226	(10%)	792	(33%)	219	(9%)	163	(7%)	92	(4%)	3.6
Non-resident	12	(1%)	127	(5%)	382	(16%)	158	(7%)	94	(4%)	60	(3%)	3.5
Age: Under 23	8	(0%)	161	(7%)	436	(18%)	128	(5%)	114	(5%)	60	(3%)	3.6
23-25	15	(1%)	104	(4%)	403	(17%)	124	(5%)	87	(4%)	45	(2%)	3.6
26-28	12	(1%)	29	(1%)	122	(5%)	51	(2%)	20	(1%)	22	(1%)	3.5
29-31	9	(0%)	18	(1%)	68	(3%)	24	(1%)	17	(1%)	9	(0%)	3.5
32-34	1	(0%)	6	(0%)	42	(2%)	21	(1%)	11	(0%)	4	(0%)	3.4
Over 34	13	(1%)	37	(2%)	103	(4%)	31	(1%)	7	(0%)	12	(1%)	3.8
Current Status: Undergraduate	14	(1%)	242	(10%)	788	(33%)	232	(10%)	188	(8%)	111	(5%)	3.6
Graduate	44	(2%)	112	(5%)	385	(16%)	147	(6%)	69	(3%)	41	(2%)	3.6
While Pursuing this Degree, Did You: (Undergraduates)													
Originally Enroll at Ole Miss	5	(0%)	152	(10%)	443	(28%)	134	(9%)	113	(7%)	65	(4%)	3.6
Transfer from 2-Yr. Institution	3	(0%)	53	(3%)	217	(14%)	66	(4%)	54	(3%)	31	(2%)	3.5
Transfer from 4-Yr. Institution	4	(0%)	35	(2%)	122	(8%)	30	(2%)	18	(1%)	15	(1%)	3.7
Undergraduate Degree from: (Graduate and Law)													
Ole Miss	9	(1%)	38	(5%)	134	(19%)	49	(7%)	25	(3%)	12	(2%)	3.6
Other Institution	30	(4%)	65	(9%)	217	(30%)	83	(11%)	37	(5%)	25	(3%)	3.6
Years Attended Ole Miss: 1	2	(0%)	12	(1%)	32	(1%)	9	(0%)	6	(0%)	1	(0%)	3.8
2	18	(1%)	63	(3%)	222	(9%)	66	(3%)	46	(2%)	30	(1%)	3.6
3	18	(1%)	57	(2%)	215	(9%)	70	(3%)	49	(2%)	26	(1%)	3.5
4	3	(0%)	118	(5%)	365	(16%)	89	(4%)	80	(3%)	45	(2%)	3.6
5	8	(0%)	65	(3%)	191	(8%)	81	(3%)	52	(2%)	30	(1%)	3.5
6+	7	(0%)	39	(2%)	127	(5%)	56	(2%)	22	(1%)	17	(1%)	3.6
GPA (Estimated): 3.75-4.00	22	(1%)	77	(3%)	241	(10%)	96	(4%)	46	(2%)	25	(1%)	3.6
3.50-3.74	9	(0%)	56	(2%)	177	(8%)	58	(3%)	39	(2%)	21	(1%)	3.6
3.25-3.49	5	(0%)	42	(2%)	148	(6%)	35	(2%)	35	(2%)	17	(1%)	3.6
3.00-3.24	8	(0%)	56	(2%)	214	(9%)	66	(3%)	44	(2%)	30	(1%)	3.5
2.75-2.99	5	(0%)	39	(2%)	136	(6%)	46	(2%)	26	(1%)	15	(1%)	3.6
2.50-2.74	6	(0%)	36	(2%)	92	(4%)	28	(1%)	34	(1%)	15	(1%)	3.5
2.25-2.49	1	(0%)	29	(1%)	86	(4%)	24	(1%)	9	(0%)	15	(1%)	3.6
2.00-2.24	0	(0%)	14	(1%)	49	(2%)	14	(1%)	10	(0%)	12	(1%)	3.4
1.99 or Less	1	(0%)	0	(0%)	3	(0%)	0	(0%)	1	(0%)	0	(0%)	3.5
Semesters Lived in Residence Hall:													
0	42	(2%)	131	(6%)	514	(22%)	147	(6%)	87	(4%)	58	(2%)	3.6
1	3	(0%)	42	(2%)	124	(5 %)	46	(2%)	42	(2%)	20	(1%)	3.5
2	7	(0%)	86	(4%)	258	(11%)	82	(3%)	51	(2%)	30	(1%)	3.6
3	1	(0%)	24	(1%)	54	(2%)	26	(1%)	10	(0%)	10	(0%)	3.6
4	1	(0%)	47	(2%)	133	(6%)	41	(2%)	29	(1%)	19	(1%)	3.6
5+	2	(0%)	20	(1%)	81	(3%)	33	(1%)	37	(2%)	13	(1%)	3.3
Fraternity/Sorority Member: Yes	3	(0%)	122	(5%)	268	(11%)	80	(3%)	52	(2%)	37	(2%)	3.7
No	51	(2%)	225	(10%)	902	(38%)	295	(13%)	203	(9%)	112	(5%)	3.5
Average Hours Employed Per Week:													
0	12	(1%)	123	(5%)	333	(15%)	93	(4%)	62	(3%)	34	(2%)	3.7
1-10	4	(0%)	47	(2%)	154	(7%)	55	(2%)	38	(2%)	22	(1%)	3.5
11-20	10	(0%)	66	(3%)	285	(13%)	106	(5%)	68	(3%)	48	(2%)	3.4
21-30	3	(0%)	31	(1%)	126	(6%)	60	(3%)	42	(2%)	23	(1%)	3.4
31-40	6	(0%)	25	(1%)	85	(4%)	25	(1%)	19	(1%)	12	(1%)	3.6
40+	22	(1%)	37	(2%)	127	(6%)	21	(1%)	18	(1%)	9	(0%)	3.8

**1 = Very Unsatisfied, 2 = Unsatisfied, 3 = Neutral, 4 = Satisfied, 5 = Very Satisfied

provide information specifically focused on the services of the unit to various types of students (see, e.g., Figure 21). Listings of commercially available graduating student and enrolled student surveys are shown in Figure 22.

Figure 22

Commercial Surveys of Current or Graduating Student Satisfaction
American College Testing (ACT)
Entering Student Survey
Student Opinion Survey
Student Opinion Survey (Two-Year)
College Outcomes Survey
Withdrawing/Non-Returning Student Survey
Withdrawing/Non-Returning Student Survey (Short Form)
Educational Testing Services (ETS)
Program Self-Assessment Service (PSAS)
Currently Enrolled Students
Graduate Program Self-Assessment Services (GPSAS)
Currently Enrolled Students
Student Reactions to College (Four-Year)
Student Reactions to College (Two-Year)
Institutional Functioning Inventory
College-Bound/National Center for Higher Education Management Systems (Student Outcomes Information System or SOIS)
Entering Student Questionnaire (Four-Year)
Entering Student Questionnaire (Two-Year)
Continuing Student Questionnaire (Four-Year)
Continuing Student Questionnaire (Two-Year)
Program Completer and Graduating Student Questionnaire (Four-Year)
Program Completer and Graduating Student Questionnaire (Two-Year)
Noel-Levits (USA Group)
Student Satisfaction Survey Inventory

The inclusion of client satisfaction items on surveys of alumni also frequently takes place. This is probably warranted, if not advisable, especially for services utilized by alumni (Alumni Department, Career Center, Publications, Development, etc.), but alumni recollections of other administrative and educational support unit services (Financial Aid, Registration, Intramural Sports, Library, etc.) have diminished over time and are not terribly useful. Also, many of these units may have changed or improved their services dramatically since responding alumni were students. Most alumni surveys focus upon reports of alumni accomplishments since graduation or other more instructionally focused items as shown in Figure 23. Standardized alumni surveys are produced by a number of vendors and include those shown in Figure 24.

Institutional employees represent the final constituency served by AES units of the institution. Institutional employees are provided services by Physical Plant, Campus Security, Human Resources, Payroll, Media Services, and a number of other units. While not as frequent, it is not unusual for institutions to conduct

Figure 23

The University of Mississippi
Undergraduate Alumni Survey

This survey concerns the degree and major indicated below which you recently received from The University of Mississippi. Even if you have received an additional degree, please focus your responses for the degree indicated. List any corrections for degree and major in the blanks provided. The number code on the label below is designed only for office follow-up on nonreturned surveys to ensure a representative response for all majors of the University.

Degree (e.g., B.A.)	Field of Study (e.g., English)	Year Degree Conferred

For Office Use Only
① ②

In which type of degree program have you enrolled since receiving the degree indicated on the label?

   ① I have not enrolled in a degree program.
   ② I have enrolled in another undergraduate degree program.
   ③ I have enrolled in a master's degree program
   ④ I have enrolled in a professional degree program (e.g., J.D., Pharm.D., M.D.)
   ⑤ I have enrolled in a doctoral degree program.

   Please provide information about the institution in which you are enrolled for this degree.
   Institution Name _____ City _____ State _____

Have you taken a professional examination related to your major since graduating from The University of Mississippi? ① Yes **Did you pass the examination?** ① Yes
  ② No   ② No

   Please enter the name of the examination. _____

Have you become licensed or certified since graduating from The University of Mississippi? ① Yes
  ② No

   In what area have you become licensed or certified? _____ *When?* _____

Please darken the oval indicating the extent to which you agree or disagree with each of the following statements.

	strongly agree	agree	neutral	disagree	strongly disagree	not applicable
The curriculum for my degree was relevant to the position I now hold.	⑤	④	③	②	①	⊛
I would recommend Ole Miss to other students.	⑤	④	③	②	①	⊛
I would recommend my undergraduate degree program to other students.	⑤	④	③	②	①	⊛
My undergraduate experience at The University of Mississippi…						
prepared me for graduate study in my major field.	⑤	④	③	②	①	⊛
prepared me for professional employment in my field.	⑤	④	③	②	①	⊛
enabled me to compete effectively with colleagues educated elsewhere.	⑤	④	③	②	①	⊛
While attending The University of Mississippi…						
I acquired the skills necessary for success in my field.	⑤	④	③	②	①	⊛
I obtained the knowledge necessary for success in my field.	⑤	④	③	②	①	⊛
I received good career advising from my department.	⑤	④	③	②	①	⊛
I gained the ability to understand issues of general social and political interest.	⑤	④	③	②	①	⊛
I learned to analyze and evaluate competing or contradictory information or points of view on topics.	⑤	④	③	②	①	⊛
I developed the ability to write effectively.	⑤	④	③	②	①	⊛
I developed the ability to express myself effectively through speaking.	⑤	④	③	②	①	⊛
I developed good listening skills.	⑤	④	③	②	①	⊛
I developed the ability to understand the relationship between skill/knowledge and the obligation to use that skill/knowledge ethically.	⑤	④	③	②	①	⊛

For Office Use Only
① ⓪ ⓪ ⓪
② ① ① ①
③ ② ② ②
④ ③ ③ ③
⑤ ④ ④ ④
⑥ ⑤ ⑤ ⑤
⑦ ⑥ ⑥ ⑥
⑦ ⑦ ⑦
⑧ ⑧ ⑧
⑨ ⑨ ⑨

When were you offered the first full-time position you held after graduation?

   ① I have not yet obtained a full-time position.
   ② I secured employment before graduation.
   ③ 1-3 months after graduation.
   ④ 4-6 months after graduation.
   ⑤ 7-9 months after graduation.
   ⑥ 10-12 months after graduation.

How many job offers did you receive before accepting your first position after graduation?
  ① 0 - 3
  ② 4 - 6
  ③ 7 - 9
  ④ more than 10

Page Two
Continue Figure 23
Current Employment Questions:

How did you learn of your present position?

① I worked with the employer before graduation.
② The University of Mississippi Career Center
③ Employment agency
④ Newspaper advertisement
⑤ Faculty contact or reference
⑥ Personal contact
⑦ I am currently not employed.
⑧ Other _____

What are you currently doing?
(Mark all that apply.)

① I am working full-time for pay.
② I am working part-time for pay.
③ I am working without compensation.
④ I am pursuing further education.
⑤ I am unemployed and looking for a position.
⑥ I am unemployed and not looking for a position.

If you are currently not working for pay, why not?

① I chose not to enter the workforce at this time.
② It has been difficult to find a position in my field.
③ It has been difficult to find a position paying an appropriate salary.

Indicate the range of your beginning salary (Optional)

① Under $25,000
② $25,000 - $35,000
③ $35,000 - $45,000
④ $45,000 - $55,000
⑤ Over $55,000

What is the company name of your current employer? _____ What is your job title? _____

What is your employment address?_____ City_____ State _____

While attending The University of Mississippi, did you...

Yes	No	
Ⓨ	Ⓝ	register with the Career Center?
Ⓨ	Ⓝ	receive assistance with writing your resume from the Career Center?
Ⓨ	Ⓝ	develop a job search plan with the assistance from the Career Center staff?
Ⓨ	Ⓝ	receive information on interview techniques from the Career Center?
Ⓨ	Ⓝ	interview for employment through the Career Center?

Please darken the oval indicating your response to the questions concerning the Alumni Association.

Yes	No	
Ⓨ	Ⓝ	Did you receive your free membership in the Alumni Association when you graduated?
Ⓨ	Ⓝ	Did you accept the $10 special alumni membership offered for your second year following graduation?
Ⓨ	Ⓝ	Have you attended your local alumni club meeting?
Ⓨ	Ⓝ	Have you visited the Alumni Association's webpage: www.alum.olemiss.edu?
Ⓨ	Ⓝ	Do you plan to become involved in alumni activities?

What is your gender?

① Female
② Male

What is your ethnicity?
① African American
② Asian/Pacific Islander
③ Caucasian
④ Hispanic American
⑤ Native American
⑥ Other_____

What was your approximate final G.P.A.?

① 2.00 - 2.50
② 2.51 - 3.00
③ 3.01 - 3.50
④ 3.51 - 4.00

Please use the space below to write comments regarding your University of Mississippi undergraduate experience.

_____

_____

THANK YOU for your response!!! Please return survey in envelope provided by January 17, 2000.

Alumni Survey, The University of Mississippi, 217 Martindale Center, University, MS 38655

Figure 24

Commercial Surveys of Alumni Satisfaction

American College Testing

  Alumni Survey

  Alumni Survey (Two-Year)

  Alumni Outcomes Survey

Educational Testing Services

  Program Self-Assessment Service (PSAS) Recent Alumni

  Graduate Program Self-Assessment Services (GPSAS)

   Recent Alumni

  Institutional Functioning Inventory

College Board/National Center for Higher Education Management Systems(Student Outcomes Information System or SOIS)

  Recent Alumni Questionnaire (Four-Year)

  Recent Alumni Questionnaire (Two-Year)

  Long-Term Alumni Questionnaire (Four-Year)

  Long-Term Alumni Questionnaire (Two-Year)

Figure 25

Commercial Surveys of Employee Satisfaction

Educational Testing Services - (ETS)

  Program Self-Assessment Service (PSAS) - Faculty

  Graduate Program Self-Assessment Services (GPSAS) - Faculty

  Institutional Functioning Inventory - Faculty and Staff

Performance Horizons Consulting Groups

  Campus Quality Survey-Faculty and Staff

---

periodic surveys of their employees concerning the services provided by administrative units. Such surveys of employees are frequently conducted as part of the institutional self-study in preparation for regional accreditation reaffirmation. On other occasions, employees are asked to express their satisfaction with unit services by completion of standardized employee/faculty surveys such as those listed in Figure 25. In a growing number of states, these are required for accountability purposes. As you will note in a number of instances, these instruments are identical to those provided for currently enrolled students/graduates and alumni. Vendors frequently compare and contrast the views of each of these groups of clientele concerning institutional services.

Each of these types of general or institutional level surveys (enrolled and/or graduating students, alumni, and employees) described provides good *preliminary* assessment of overall client satisfaction with unit services. However, unless detailed questions concerning satisfaction with unit services are included on these general questionnaires (a circumstance exceedingly rare due to the need to keep institutional level surveys brief), they serve only to raise a flag or to question those unit services where overall client satisfaction is not what the unit thinks it ought to be. This question will need to be resolved by more detailed analysis of unit services through means such as the point of contact survey discussed next.

Use of Point-of-Contact Surveys by Administrative and Educational Support Units

Detailed and specific information concerning client satisfaction with unit services is normally obtained through a "point-of-contact" survey distributed and collected at the time the client receives the services. The purpose of the survey is to ascertain in greater depth or detail the satisfaction of the client with particular aspects of the services provided. An example of such point-of-contact survey regarding library services is provided as Figure 26.

The point-of-contact survey is conducted under three types of circumstances. First, distribution of point-of-contact surveys can be a routine form of unit assessment activities. Second, point-of-contact surveys can be initiated when the unit feels that some aspect of its operations is not performing in the manner "it ought to perform" and desires more information concerning client satisfaction with this aspect of services. However, the most common reason for initiating point-of-contact surveys is to measure client satisfaction with unit services that have been found to be less than desirable in the overall or institutional survey.

Point-of-contact surveys exhibit a number of advantages. They can be detailed enough to provide specific information that will lead the unit to direct corrective action. Also, the unit receives virtually instant feedback from clients as they tabulate the results of point-of-contact surveys and can immediately put a "fix in place" now, rather than later in the year. Finally, because they were involved in the design of the survey, the unit staff normally attach a great deal of creditability to the results of such findings.

Figure 26

LIBRARY SATISFACTION SURVEY

Please help us improve library service by answering
a few questions about TODAY's visit

1. What did you do in the library **today**?
For each activity, *circle the number* that best reflects how satisfied you were with the outcome.

Satisfaction

	Did not do today	Very dissatisfied				Very Satisfied
Looked for books	0	1	2	3	4	5
Looked for periodicals	0	1	2	3	4	5
Used course reserves	0	1	2	3	4	5
Used on-line library catalog	0	1	2	3	4	5
Asked a reference question	0	1	2	3	4	5
Used electronic database						
(InfoTRAC, FirstSearch, ERIC, etc.)	0	1	2	3	4	5
Used media/microforms equipment	0	1	2	3	4	5
Used copy machine	0	1	2	3	4	5
Browsed	0	1	2	3	4	5
Studied	0	1	2	3	4	5

2. If you received assistance from library staff, how satisfied were you
with the service? *(Circle one)*:

Very dissatisfied				Very satisfied
1	2	3	4	5

Why?_____

3. Overall, how <u>satisfied</u> are you with <u>today's</u> library visit? *(Circle one)*:

Very dissatisfied				Very satisfied
1	2	3	4	5

Why?_____

4. You are *(check one)*:

____1. Undergraduate ____2. Graduate student ____3. Faculty ____4. Staff ____5. Visitor

5. Your major or department: _____

6. What would you like to see improved in the library? Please use the back of this form for your response and any other comments. Thanks.

There are two major limitations concerning point-of-contact surveys, the time required for construction and administration of the surveys, and a tendency toward over surveying of the student population.

The amount of time necessary to design, produce, distribute, and tabulate the results of a point-of-contact survey should not be underestimated. It can have a substantial impact on a unit's ability to provide services during the period of the survey. An emerging development in the field of unit-level point-of-contact client satisfaction measures is the availability of specific nationally standardized surveys regarding different fields. These surveys both save AES unit effort and provide normative data. Examples of these are the Residents' Satisfaction and R.A. Benchmarking Survey conducted by the Association of College and University Housing Officers International in conjunction with Educational Benchmarking, Inc., and the Quality and Importance of Recreational Services Survey developed in conjunction with the National Intramural-Recreational Sports Association related to the field of intramural athletics. It is anticipated that more of this type of nationally standardized survey regarding a particular field may become available in the future.

Among the greatest survey research problems which a unit or the institution needs to guard against is the over surveying of the student population. The authors can recall one experience when they were visiting an institution where a hotel was operated on the campus as part of the Hotel Management instructional program. A point-of-contact survey was distributed as part of the hotel registration process to ascertain guest satisfaction with the registration procedures. In the room, another point-of-contact survey was administered to ascertain satisfaction with the facility and its cleanliness. In the restaurant operated by the hotel, there was another point-of-contact survey found under the dinner plate soliciting the customers satisfaction with the meal and service. Frankly, the authors expected point-of-contact surveys in the hotel's public restrooms. The point is simple. If the population is over surveyed, the response rate will decline, and before that, the sincerity of the responses will diminish significantly as respondents begin to mark all of one response (for example, all of #3) or "satisfied." There needs to be institutional coordination (possibly through the institutional research component) which limits the number of point-of-contact surveys which are conducted each semester or quarter so the student population will not be over surveyed.

This tendency to over survey student populations is a reflection of the general tendency on the part of AES units to over emphasize or rely on survey research (particularly point-of-contact) as their primary means of assessment. Units need to ask themselves each time they consider a survey, "Is there another way to do this assessment without having to ask the clients?" Given a bit of imagination, it is amazing how many other sources of information are available. As an example, were the Office of Student Housing to identify an administrative objective related to the provision of a safe environment for its residents, instead of soliciting their opinion (perception) regarding the safety of their environment, the department could justifiably rely upon, (a) the number of campus police and fire department calls, (b) the number of citations given by the fire marshal, (c) reports of security checks concerning exterior doors, etc., as alternative means of assessment. On the other hand, were the administrative objective to relate to the occupant's belief that he or she resided in a safe environment, an attitudinal survey would be the most appropriate means of assessment.

Another means of identifying appropriate questions for each service unit is to contact similar service units at peer institutions to determine what they have utilized. "Survey swaps" are not common, but occasionally transpire at professional meetings.

Improving the Credibility of Survey Research as a Means of Assessment in AES Units

The credibility of the survey research described is dependent upon the nature of the questions asked, the conditions under which they are answered, and the overall response rate. The respondents should be given the opportunity to relate their satisfaction with the services provided on a continuum (four or five point) scale. In addition, the respondents should be able to indicate if a particular service is "not applicable" or was not used in their experience at the institution. As an example, it would be inappropriate for commuting students to indicate their satisfaction with residence hall programming.

The conditions under which respondents complete satisfaction surveys also clearly influences the nature of their responses. Respondents should be given the opportunity to complete questionnaires in an anonymous manner without concern for identification of their individual response. Given such anonymity, it has been the authors' experience that students/graduates and alumni are clearly willing to provide their candid, forthright, and often highly complimentary opinions or dissatisfaction with essential college and university services.

The survey response rate has a bearing on the overall creditability of client satisfaction measures. This rate is influenced primarily by the nature of the recipients and the manner in which the questionnaire is distributed. If at all possible, avoid mailing questionnaires as response rates suffer significantly. Alternatives to mailing include insertion of questionnaires into administrative processing (such as the process for applying for graduation) or having captive audiences such as classes, alumni meetings, advisory boards, etc., complete these measures prior to departure from a setting. Once a questionnaire is placed in the mail, the respondent has more of an opportunity to "just forget it" than if the questionnaire is included within a process or meeting context. In all cases, (distribution within a process, meeting, or mail), response rates less than 70%, while undesirable in a classic research setting, may be acceptable for assessment purposes. When faced with such low response rates, the AES unit must give careful consideration to the consistency of the responses received and potential for response bias. However, if the responses received consistently identify the same problems (thus identifying trends) with a particular aspect of unit services, response rates as low as 20-30% may provide the unit with cause for action or at the very least, further inquiry.

The final issue in survey research credibility on a campus relates to the quality of the survey instrumentation and its source. While only the AES units involved can identify the appropriate questions to which clientele should respond, most AES units are not adept at survey design. Many well-intentioned units, design and distribute questionnaires which fail to ask questions in such a manner as to objectively elicit the needed feedback in a systematic manner suitable for analysis. Additionally, these units often take valuable time from their current services to provide questionnaires whose appearance is not that which the institution wishes to portray to its public. Therefore, it is the recommendation of the authors that the institution establish a centralized service to assist AES units, as well as academic programs in the design of surveys for assessment purposes. This service is normally provided by the institutional research component using the hardware and software described in Appendix C. Establishment of this service will:

- Ease the burden on AES units of the design of surveys.
- Provide central data analysis support.
- Result in better appearance of the surveys.
- Serve to coordinate client satisfaction surveys (thereby avoiding over surveying the population).

Direct Measures as a Means of Assessment for AES Units

An excellent means of assessment for AES units is the direct measure of unit accomplishments. This primarily consists of a simple count of unit activities and is the second most common form of assessment in administrative and educational support units.

Direct counts as means of assessment are usually found in records maintained in the AES unit. The use of direct measures often *requires* the unit to already have available the data from a previous assessment period with which to compare current or future assessment results. In this case, the unit administrative objective will have been stated in such a way that some level of improvement will be shown between the two assessment periods of time referenced.

Shown in Figure 27 are common direct or simple measures. In most cases, these data already exist in unit records or the institution's data system. In other cases, these data (such as cost per applicant, vouchers processed per clerk, etc.) will need to be freshly created from institutional operational data combined with financial and human resource information. Examples of these types of data are shown in Figure 28. The major advantage of these data is the unit's ability to compare its efficiency or productivity with either a peer group of institutions or a national sample. Hence, the administrative objective for a particular AES unit might be that unit cost or time processing vendor statements would be either at or below the national or peer group average. The means of assessment cited would be the comparative data element in the annual benchmarking study. The ability to make these normative comparisons enhances the value of direct measurement of unit performance by providing comparison information.

A particularly interesting set of direct measures (from which Figure 28 was

Figure 27

Examples of Direct Measures
of AES Unit Effectiveness

- Admissions ———————— Application Response Timing
- Admissions ———————— Telephone Response Timing
- Business Affairs ———————— Monitoring Grants & Contracts
- Campus Security ———————— Availability of Parking
- Dean of Students———————— Room Assignments
- Development ———————— Mailing List Development
- Food Services ———————— Cafeteria Service
- Human Resources ———————— Selection Processes
- Plant Operations ———————— Work Order Response
- Physical Plant ———————— Remodeling Process
- Printing Services ———————— Bulk Mail Distribution
- Printing Services ———————— Reduction of Pre-Press Time
- Registrar's Office ———————— Grade Posting
- Registrar's Office ———————— Clearing Transcript Holds
- Treasurer's Office ———————— Payroll Distribution

Figure 28

Example National Association of College
and University Business Officers' (NACUBO)
Normative Comparisons for the
Registration Functions

- Percent Anytime Classroom Occupancy

- Average Class Size (Following Data in Days)

- Average Turnaround Time to Process Official
  Transcript Request

- Average Turnaround Time to Process Student
  Enrollment Verification Request

- Average Turnaround Time to Process Grade
  Reports

- Average Turnaround Time to Process
  Graduation Eligibility Determination

drawn) concerning unit efficiency can be gained by taking part in the National Association of College and University Business Officers (NACUBO) annual benchmarking project. This project provides a number of data elements related to the volume and efficiency of many educational support and administrative units on a campus and can be expanded to measures of client satisfaction.

External Evaluation as a Form of AES Service Assessment

In countless examples, external evaluators already periodically render reports (which can be readily used for assessment purposes) regarding the operations of various AES units. These external evaluations constitute periodic assessments of the relationship of the unit's operations to "good and acceptable practices in the field," by a neutral party. These reviews can provide an excellent source of assessment information with little effort or cost on the part of the AES unit. This is particularly helpful for campuses with a very limited number of administrative staff available for doing assessment activities. Examples of these types of external validation or review are the Auditor's report concerning the institution's financial condition and processes, the Fire Marshal's report following inspection of facilities, the Health Department's report after inspection of the food service facility, etc. In each case, the responsible administrative and educational support unit need only incorporate the results of this already scheduled external evaluation into its means of assessment.

Upon other occasions, an AES unit may wish to incorporate into its assessment plan the use of an external consultant specifically employed for the purpose of evaluating unit operations and making recommendations for improvement. However, no *requirement* for the use of external consultants exists. The employment of an external consultant should not be sought because a unit "seems to be in trouble" or the staff in the unit will move from service improvement to protection of the individuals within the unit.

Units may select external consultants as evaluators from near and far. For little or no cost, administrative personnel in similar capacities at peer institutions often serve one another as consultant/evaluators. Professional associations also have in many cases established registers of qualified consultants in their field. On a considerably smaller scale, the authors are aware of a small college that asked a local janitorial service (which provided service to the local public schools) to come to its campus and evaluate the cleanliness of the college's buildings. The local janitorial service was delighted to be asked and provided such evaluation at no cost to the institution.

The primary disadvantages to the use of external evaluators or consultants are their identification and the cost of their remuneration. When using those external evaluators that come to the campus as part of their employment (auditor, fire marshal, etc.), one of these problems is solved. However, the institution is bound to the standard set by the agency employing the external evaluator. The other disadvantage, cost of external evaluator remuneration, can vary from nearly nothing to a substantial amount. In general, those external evaluators drawn from locations geographically near the college will cost less and from more distant locations or with national reputations in the field, more.

Assessment of "Outcome Oriented" Administrative Objectives

A number of the AES units at an institution (normally described as educational support in nature) measure the skills gained by clients to validate their unit's accomplishments. Many educational support units provide these services through which students gain required knowledge and skills (outcomes). To validate these educational support units' accomplishments, it is necessary to measure the clients' (normally students) ability after the provision of these services (see Figure 29). In the Library, this includes instruction

Figure 29

Examples of Outcome Measures for AES Units

Intended Client Outcome	Means of Assessment
1. Students will write an acceptable resume.	1. Observations by recruiters
2. Students will understand the concept of cultural diversity.	2. Workshop Pre-Test/Post-Test by staff
3. Staff will utilize the Human Resources on-line query system to trace their employment requests.	3. Observation of Human Resources Internet hit count by Human Resources Staff
4. Students will be able to use bibliographical references.	4. Performance assessment by Library staff
5. Graduates will gain an appreciation of fine arts.	5. Count of Fine Arts Series attendance by Artist Series staff.
6. Parents will recognize the importance of student immunizations.	6. Observation of Student Health records by clinical staff
7. Graduates will conduct themselves "professionally" during job interviews.	7. Performance assessment by companies participating in Career Fair
8. Students will be responsible citizens.	8. Observation of participation in student elections by Student Life Staff

concerning utilization of library resources resulting in the ability of the students to do scholarly research. Information Technology frequently provides instructional services regarding basic computer operations, Internet access, utilization of software programs, etc. This instruction enables students to use the campus computer facilities as part of their learning process. Much work in the Career Center has to do with training students regarding resume preparation, the job search, and interview techniques. Performance, observation, and cognitive pre-test/post-test are common means of student outcomes assessment utilized by AES units. In these cases, AES units will need to utilize means similar to those used in the campus instructional programs and described in the third edition of *The Departmental Guide and Record Book for Student Outcomes Assessment and Institutional Effectiveness* now available from Agathon Press. Essentially, these relate to measurement of the knowledge or skills acquired by the clients. Fortunately, most such skills transmitted by AES units are fairly straightforward and their measurement is readily apparent from the services provided.

In educational support and administrative units, while the means of assessment are normally limited to client satisfaction, direct measures or counts, and external evaluation, and in some cases, student outcomes assessment, they are among the most visible and key steps in establishing the AES unit's assessment plan. Once the means of assessment are identified, they facilitate the establishment of the AES unit's performance benchmark or the Criteria for Success which includes this chapter.

Step Four: An Approach That Works—Identifying Means of Assessment

Since the formulation of administrative objectives leads naturally to and dictates the means of assessment, extension of the process used to establish administrative objectives supports this relationship. The establishment of administrative objectives was described earlier as taking probably two staff meetings. It is a rather easy matter to extend the second meeting concerning administrative objectives to introduce the subject of means of assessment for those objectives. After the administrative objectives have been clearly identified in the second staff meeting, ask the staff to address the question, "What will provide for us the information necessary to see that these objectives are being met?" This question leads naturally into the identification of the means of assessment for each of the objectives. Within one, perhaps two, more staff meetings, each of the means of assessment can be further described and the staff lead to consideration of the criteria for their success.

Establishment of the "Unit Criteria Success" in AES Units

An often overlooked step in the process of establishing an assessment plan for an administrative or educational support service (AES) unit is that of identifying a reasonable level of service improvement to expect given the resources and personnel the unit has available. Establishing a level identifies in the eyes of the AES unit how well they "ought" to serve their clientele. If a level or "criteria for success" is not established prior to the reporting of the assessment results, everyone simply says, "That is about what I thought the results should be," and they go about their business with little or no stretch for improvement of services. Establishing a specific indicator for accomplishment of the administrative objective (criteria for success), creates a cohesive target for the staff and an interest and excitement in the assessment process. There is no stronger motivational tool to get staff to use the results of assessment activities for service improvement (the essential intent of what all that precedes is attempting to accomplish) than their setting a "criteria for success" or benchmark for client satisfaction.

Criteria for success are often set at both the *primary* (overall) and *secondary* (detailed) levels as reference points or benchmarks for unit performance. *Primary* criteria for success establish overall targets for unit performance such as "95% of students completing a point-of-contact survey will be "very satisfied" or "satisfied" with their "overall experience" with the Career Center. The potential use of results for service improvement can be *greatly enhanced* by also setting more detailed criteria for success which require *secondary* analysis such as "and no less than 80% of respondents will rate any single item on the point-of-contact survey similarly." While overall unit performance may meet or exceed the primary criteria for success, staff are informed through consideration of this secondary analysis of those more specific areas, scales, or individual items falling short of their expectations. Whenever feasible, staff should set not only primary, but secondary criteria for success and conduct detailed analysis of assessment information to the level necessary for it to be of use.

There are several means through which an AES unit can establish realistic criteria for success. First, the unit can use an alternative scenario approach. With this approach, the unit selects a percentage of improvement for its service that they would like to see. Next, the staff discuss what they would think of their services if the services reached that level. The staff then chooses two other percentages usually one higher and one lower than the original and discusses these choices. Discussions of this type lead the staff to select a percentage of improvement with which they are comfortable and believe realistic given the resources and personnel available to the unit.

Second, looking to one's peers can help identify realistic criteria in some instances. A technique that works very well on many campuses, particularly where one person provides the service, is that of using peer institutions. Calling an individual at a peer institution who is providing the same service and discussing administrative objectives will often help identify a realistic criterion for the provision of that particular service. The information provided by peers is invaluable and is provided at no cost to the institution. Remember that these institutions are involved in the same process and will probably want your ideas as well. Many professional meetings have sessions dealing with expectations for service. Attending these sessions can provide guidelines for the establishment of your unit's criteria for success. Upon occasion, an AES unit may need to collect baseline information prior to identification of an amount for service improvement. While this is an acceptable practice, AES units need to be careful not to merely accept "what is" (the baseline data) rather than identifying "what ought to be" their criteria for service improvement.

When an administrative or educational support unit feels threatened or they are not sure how the process will work "for" or "against" them, two things often occur. First, the unit will set its criteria for success at a high level, but only assess those things they are positive are being done well. In these cases, it is not unusual to see criteria set for an administrative objective at the 90th percentile or higher. When this occurs, the question arises, "Is this really a service worth measuring for improvement?" On the other hand, the unit may set its criteria for success regarding improvement of an important service improvement so low that it is easy to accomplish and does not result in significant improvement.

Sometimes, improvement of services occurs in very small percentages or numbers. It is not unusual for significant improvements to come from reducing the period of time required for a process by as little as an hour. When this slight improvement is considered over a month's period of time, it can add several hours of staff time that can be redirected into improvement of some other specific service.

As referenced earlier concerning administrative objectives, there are two ways to win and two ways to lose when you set realistic criteria for service improvement. The first "win" is, of course, to meet your criteria for success. At that point, it's time for your staff to celebrate and publicize your success. There should be more celebrations than frustrations in assessment practice. The second way to win occurs when you do not meet your criteria for success, but instead implement procedures for further service improvements to meet your criteria at the end of the next cycle. It might seem difficult to "lose" having gone as far in assessment planning as setting a criteria for success. However, it frequently happens. The first way to lose is not to do the assessment plan. In many cases, AES units become focused on day-to-day operations and fail to carry through with their plans for assessment activities. The second type of loss is even more troubling and occurs when AES units accomplish the assessment planned, but fail to use assessment information (indicating performance less than the criteria for success) as a basis for service improvement. This can take place easily if (a) the assessment activities have been premised on additional resources being provided, (b) there is not an occasion created for the unit to review its assessment results, or (c) changes suggested by the assessment information are resisted by unit staff.

Step Four: An Approach That Works—Explaining "Criteria For Success" to Your Staff

Have each staff member complete the following sentence: "I want to be a successful................" Once that is accomplished, ask them to complete this sentence: "I know that I am successful when ...." Several individuals could answer the first question with the same objective. However, each will have a different personal indicator for reaching that objective. These personal indicators are each staff member's "Criteria for Success."

This exercise allows staff members to understand the need for establishment of the criteria and recognizes the unit's need to establish its own "Criteria for Success" regarding each administrative objective.

Concluding Comments Regarding Preparation of the Assessment Plan

This chapter has discussed the first four steps in implementation of institutional effectiveness activities in educational support and administrative units. It began with the relationship of the individual AES unit to the institutional expanded statement of institutional purpose followed by the development of the AES unit's own mission statement. Next, items concerning the selection and expression of the unit's administrative objectives were discussed. Finally, various means of assessment typically used in administrative and educational support units were reviewed. All of these actions (including the establishment of criteria for success described in the preceding section, result in formulation of an assessment plan for each administrative and educational support unit at the institution (see Figures 30-33). However, this is only the plan and the conclusion of the process, improving educational support and administrative services, is described in the next chapter dealing with the fifth and sixth steps of the suggested steps for the administrative assessment process (Figure 5, page 31). In many ways the assessment plan established is the road map to our destination, improving educational support and administrative services.

Figure 30

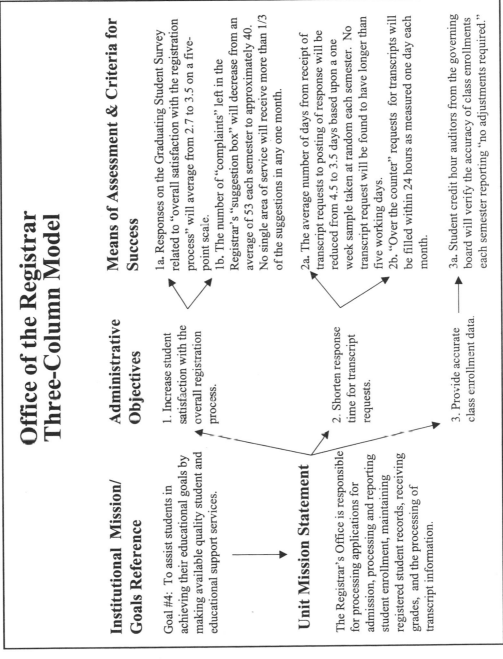

Office of the Registrar
Three-Column Model

Institutional Mission/ Goals Reference

Goal #4: To assist students in achieving their educational goals by making available quality student and educational support services.

Unit Mission Statement

The Registrar's Office is responsible for processing applications for admission, processing and reporting student enrollment, maintaining registered student records, receiving grades, and the processing of transcript information.

Administrative Objectives

1. Increase student satisfaction with the overall registration process.

2. Shorten response time for transcript requests.

3. Provide accurate class enrollment data.

Means of Assessment & Criteria for Success

1a. Responses on the Graduating Student Survey related to "overall satisfaction with the registration process" will average from 2.7 to 3.5 on a five-point scale.

1b. The number of "complaints" left in the Registrar's "suggestion box" will decrease from an average of 53 each semester to approximately 40. No single area of service will receive more than 1/3 of the suggestions in any one month.

2a. The average number of days from receipt of transcript requests to posting of response will be reduced from 4.5 to 3.5 days based upon a one week sample taken at random each semester. No transcript request will be found to have longer than five working days.

2b. "Over the counter" requests for transcripts will be filled within 24 hours as measured one day each month.

3a. Student credit hour auditors from the governing board will verify the accuracy of class enrollments each semester reporting "no adjustments required."

Figure 31

Career Center
Three-Column Model

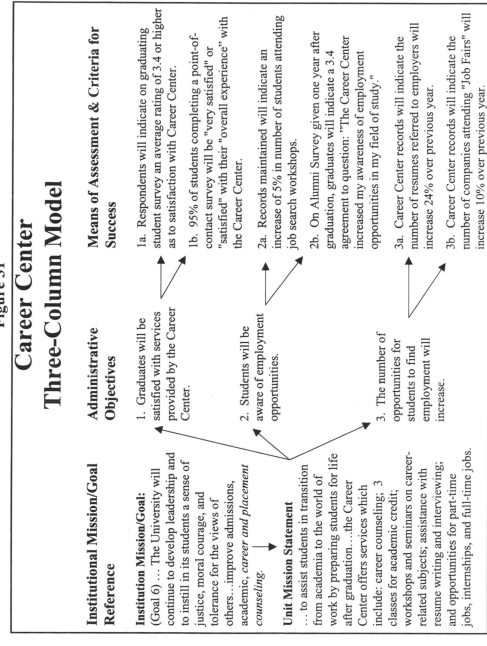

Institutional Mission/Goal Reference	Administrative Objectives	Means of Assessment & Criteria for Success
Institution Mission/Goal: (Goal 6) ... The University will continue to develop leadership and to instill in its students a sense of justice, moral courage, and tolerance for the views of others...improve admissions, *academic, career and placement counseling.*	1. Graduates will be satisfied with services provided by the Career Center.	1a. Respondents will indicate on graduating student survey an average rating of 3.4 or higher as to satisfaction with Career Center.
		1b. 95% of students completing a point-of-contact survey will be "very satisfied" or "satisfied" with their "overall experience" with the Career Center.
Unit Mission Statement ... to assist students in transition from academia to the world of work by preparing students for life after graduation....the Career Center offers services which include: career counseling; 3 classes for academic credit; workshops and seminars on career-related subjects; assistance with resume writing and interviewing; and opportunities for part-time and opportunities for part-time jobs, internships, and full-time jobs.	2. Students will be aware of employment opportunities.	2a. Records maintained will indicate an increase of 5% in number of students attending job search workshops.
		2b. On Alumni Survey given one year after graduation, graduates will indicate a 3.4 agreement to question: "The Career Center increased my awareness of employment opportunities in my field of study."
	3. The number of opportunities for students to find employment will increase.	3a. Career Center records will indicate the number of resumes referred to employers will increase 24% over previous year.
		3b. Career Center records will indicate the number of companies attending "Job Fairs" will increase 10% over previous year.

Figure 32

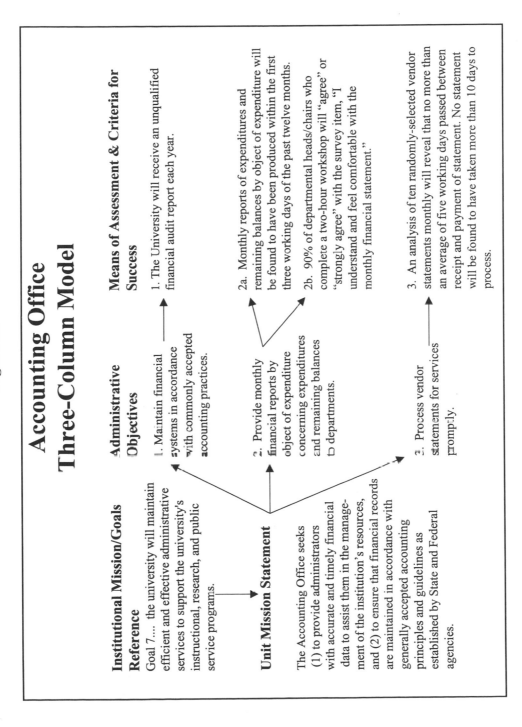

Accounting Office
Three-Column Model

Institutional Mission/Goals Reference

Goal 7.... the university will maintain efficient and effective administrative services to support the university's instructional, research, and public service programs.

Unit Mission Statement

The Accounting Office seeks (1) to provide administrators with accurate and timely financial data to assist them in the management of the institution's resources, and (2) to ensure that financial records are maintained in accordance with generally accepted accounting principles and guidelines as established by State and Federal agencies.

Administrative Objectives

1. Maintain financial systems in accordance with commonly accepted accounting practices.

2. Provide monthly financial reports by object of expenditure concerning expenditures and remaining balances to departments.

3. Process vendor statements for services promptly.

Means of Assessment & Criteria for Success

1. The University will receive an unqualified financial audit report each year.

2a. Monthly reports of expenditures and remaining balances by object of expenditure will be found to have been produced within the first three working days of the past twelve months.

2b. 90% of departmental heads/chairs who complete a two-hour workshop will "agree" or "strongly agree" with the survey item, "I understand and feel comfortable with the monthly financial statement."

3. An analysis of ten randomly-selected vendor statements monthly will reveal that no more than an average of five working days passed between receipt and payment of statement. No statement will be found to have taken more than 10 days to process.

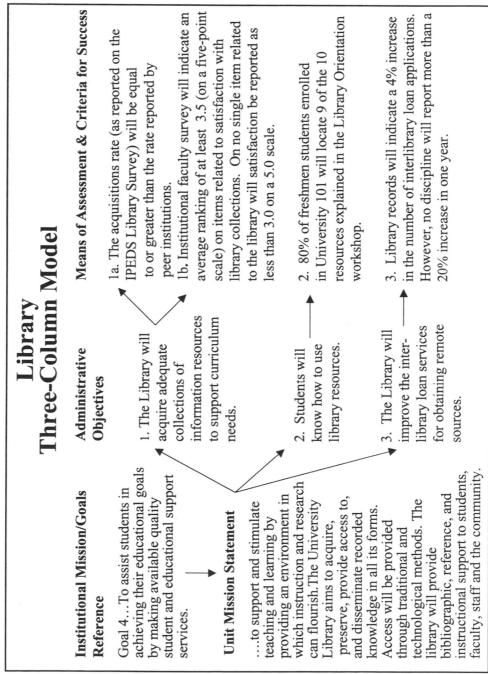

Figure 33

Library
Three-Column Model

Institutional Mission/Goals Reference

Goal 4...To assist students in achieving their educational goals by making available quality student and educational support services.

Unit Mission Statement

...to support and stimulate teaching and learning by providing an environment in which instruction and research can flourish.The University Library aims to acquire, preserve, provide access to, and disseminate recorded knowledge in all its forms. Access will be provided through traditional and technological methods. The library will provide bibliographic, reference, and instructional support to students, faculty, staff and the community.

Administrative Objectives

1. The Library will acquire adequate collections of information resources to support curriculum needs.

2. Students will know how to use library resources.

3. The Library will improve the inter-library loan services for obtaining remote sources.

Means of Assessment & Criteria for Success

1a. The acquisitions rate (as reported on the IPEDS Library Survey) will be equal to or greater than the rate reported by peer institutions.

1b. Institutional faculty survey will indicate an average ranking of at least 3.5 (on a five-point scale) on items related to satisfaction with library collections. On no single item related to the library will satisfaction be reported as less than 3.0 on a 5.0 scale.

2. 80% of freshmen students enrolled in University 101 will locate 9 of the 10 resources explained in the Library Orientation workshop.

3. Library records will indicate a 4% increase in the number of interlibrary loan applications. However, no discipline will report more than a 20% increase in one year.

CHAPTER IV

FROM PLANNING TO IMPLEMENTATION AND USE OF RESULTS

STEP FIVE—CONDUCT ASSESSMENT ACTIVITIES

Once the unit assessment plan or "Three-Column Model" has been established and approved, it will be necessary to begin implementation of these assessment activities in order to demonstrate use of results as soon as possible. Unless the unit is already conducting the assessment activities described in the unit assessment plan, it will probably take at least three to four months to fully implement most assessment plans in AES units and begin receiving useful assessment information.

Responsibility for Seeing That Assessment Gets Done

Consistent with everything else within the unit, the AES department head bears the responsibility for seeing that the assessment activities identified in the unit assessment plan are carried out. Each department head should identify which aspects of the assessment plan established are to be carried out at the institutional level and which by personnel in the unit.

When beginning the assessment of administrative objectives called for in the plan, it will pay the AES unit head to examine once more the means of assessment identified and ask the question, "Will the resulting data provide information potentially leading to improvement of unit services?" In the authors' experience, much of the assessment data collected by AES units is informative in nature, but not linked to any administrative objective or service improvement.

As indicated earlier, general or institutional level client satisfaction measures may be among the resources upon which the AES unit department head can rely. However, the AES unit department head should ensure that the *items* contained on the general or institutional level client satisfaction survey relate specifically to the administrative objectives established for the unit.

Point-of-contact client satisfaction measures, constitute the other primary means of attitudinal assessment which will require additional effort within the AES unit. Matters of timing and sampling need to be considered by the unit in execution of these point-of-contact surveys.

The AES unit will want to ensure that point-of-contact surveys are administered in such a way as to capture the opinion of the client immediately following the provision of services and before they can escape the premises. Often return of point-of-contact surveys is required when clients are making subsequent appointments, checking out a book, or returning athletic equipment. Once clients leave the unit, the rate of survey return diminishes substantially. However, in some cases, collection of the surveys before respondents leave will not be possible due to the service being completed after the client has left the AES unit. In instances such as this (exemplified by provision of athletic equipment, audio-visual material, etc.), the client will need to complete the point-of-contact survey at the time the item provided is returned.

Earlier, in Chapter Three, a strong case was made against oversampling of the population of students by AES units. Individual AES unit department heads need to determine if an institutional policy exists regarding coordination of point-of-contact surveys by AES units. Even if such a policy does not exist, point-of-contact surveys should not be administered for a prolonged period of time. Most AES units can avoid over surveying the student population by administering their attitudinal survey to every student utilizing the AES unit services two days a semester. Remember, only a representative sampling of student opinion is necessary and twice a semester should provide a sufficient sample on most campuses. A sample taken one day a week (on alternating days of the week) for six months will provide better data for assessment purposes than five weeks of consecutive questionnaire distribution and completion.

The use of direct means of assessment should also be carefully reviewed prior to actual implementation. In the case of utilization of already existing unit data for service improvement and assessment purposes, the AES unit head should look retrospectively back several years within the AES unit's data to ensure that the information required for current assessment purposes are also available in a consistent manner covering those earlier periods of time. If additional data are required for assessment purposes, the necessary collection mechanisms should be put in place. However, establishing the data collection mechanism should not itself be considered an administrative objective.

Recording the Data Collected

Assessment results should summarize the key findings of whatever means of assessment were identified. These findings should be related directly to the administrative objectives which they were designed to measure. Assessment activities which cannot be traced directly to an administrative objective require unnecessary staff hours and unit expense that could be utilized to provide service. Assessment that is not related to administrative objectives, or required for some other purpose such as state accountability measures, should be stopped.

One of the questions frequently voiced on campuses relates to "How much documentation of our assessment findings do we need to maintain?" It is not necessary to keep copies of individual questionnaires, worksheets, etc., for the entire period between reaffirmation visitations (normally ten years). The data summaries contained in the report of assessment activities suggested in Appendix A should suffice for this purpose. As a precaution, it may be advisable to keep the detailed documentation of assessment activities in the year before the team visitation takes place.

The data provided in the summary of assessment results should be complete enough to convince the reader that the assessment described actually took place. Professionals who take part in research activities (to support the summaries reported) realize that "round numbers" very rarely transpire in research endeavors. The inclusion of round numbers (unless further described as two of four, three of six, etc.) will cause the natural degree of suspicion present in many visiting team members to escalate sharply. Under these circumstances, AES unit department heads can expect to be asked to provide the actual questionnaires, spreadsheets, etc.

AES unit assessment results are the bridge between assessment plans and the unit's use of results. The assessment data collected and summarized (column 4) should logically flow from the "Means of Assessment and Criteria for Success" (column 3) described and justify the following "Use of Results" (column 5) to be described next. Without the citation of appropriate and reasonable assessment results, AES unit descriptions of the manner in which assessment results were utilized to improve services become suspect.

The Four-Column Models, the assessment plans and the recording of results through assessment results concerning the Office of the Registrar, Career Center, Accounting Office, and Library are shown in Figures 34-37 and provide a transition to the most important part of the AES unit's activities—the use of results to improve services.

STEP SIX—DOCUMENT USE OF RESULTS FOR SERVICE IMPROVEMENT

After almost a dozen years of implementation in some parts of the country, it can honestly be stated that assessment in educational support and administrative units is no longer focused upon the *act of assessment*, but upon the *use of results for service improvements*.

The use of assessment results to improve services is linked back to the unit's administrative objectives, to its Unit Mission Statement, and, ultimately, provides evidence to validate the institution's statement of purpose. This linkage through administrative objectives connects directly with regional accrediting association requirements such as those cited earlier in Figure 2 (page 16). Although meeting these regional accrediting association requirements is often the occasion for AES units initially participating in the assessment process, it is important to emphasis that the improvement of their services is the actual reason for taking part.

On the other hand, actually doing assessment and the effort to improve services frequently connects with Continuous Quality Improvement or Total Quality Management initiatives within an institution. Both of these procedures (CQI/TQM) provide a number of tools (cross-functional teams, systems analysis, etc.) for addressing the issues identified in the unit's assessment data. The difference between AES unit assessment procedures and CQI/TQM implementation is that the procedures or tools

Figure 34

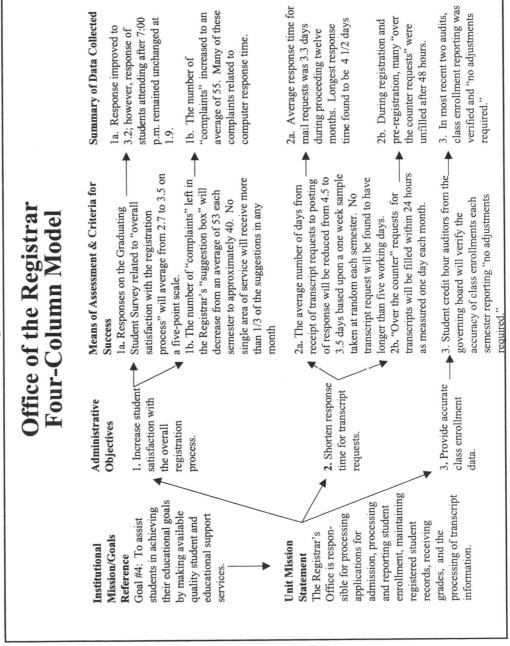

Office of the Registrar Four-Column Model

Institutional Mission/Goals Reference	Administrative Objectives	Means of Assessment & Criteria for Success	Summary of Data Collected
Goal #4: To assist students in achieving their educational goals by making available quality student and educational support services.	1. Increase student satisfaction with the overall registration process.	1a. Responses on the Graduating Student Survey related to "overall satisfaction with the registration process" will average from 2.7 to 3.5 on a five-point scale. 1b. The number of "complaints" left in the Registrar's "suggestion box" will decrease from an average of 53 each semester to approximately 40. No single area of service will receive more than 1/3 of the suggestions in any month	1a. Response improved to 3.2; however, response of students attending after 7:00 p.m. remained unchanged at 1.9. 1b. The number of "complaints" increased to an average of 55. Many of these complaints related to computer response time.
Unit Mission Statement The Registrar's Office is responsible for processing applications for admission, processing and reporting student enrollment, maintaining registered student records, receiving grades, and the processing of transcript information.	**2.** Shorten response time for transcript requests.	2a. The average number of days from receipt of transcript requests to posting of response will be reduced from 4.5 to 3.5 days based upon a one week sample taken at random each semester. No transcript request will be found to have longer than five working days. 2b. "Over the counter" requests for transcripts will be filled within 24 hours as measured one day each month.	2a. Average response time for mail requests was 3.3 days during proceeding twelve months. Longest response time found to be 4 1/2 days 2b. During registration and pre-registration, many "over the counter requests" were unfilled after 48 hours.
	3. Provide accurate class enrollment data.	3. Student credit hour auditors from the governing board will verify the accuracy of class enrollments each semester reporting "no adjustments required."	3. In most recent two audits, class enrollment reporting was verified and "no adjustments required."

Figure 35

Career Center
Four-Column Model

Institutional Mission/Goal Reference	Administrative Objectives	Means of Assessment & Criteria for Success	Summary of Data Collected
Institution Mission/Goal: (Goal 6) … The University will continue to develop leadership and to instill in its students a sense of justice, moral courage, and tolerance for the views of others …improve admissions, *academic, career and placement counseling.*	1. Graduates will be satisfied with services provided by the Career Center.	1a. Respondents will indicate on graduating student survey an average rating of 3.4 or higher as to satisfaction with Career Center. 1b. 95% of students completing a point-of-contact survey will be "very satisfied" or "satisfied" with their "overall experience" with the Career Center. On no individual item (10 items) will more than 10% of students respond "dissatisfied" or "very dissatisfied".	1a. Graduates rated satisfaction with Career Center as 3.4 However, the international students only gave a 1.4 satisfaction rating. 1b. 63% of students completing a point-of-contact survey indicated satisfaction with "overall experience" with Career Center. Most dissatisfaction was expressed in availability of access to technical career sources (34%).
Unit Mission Statement: … to assist students in transition from academia to the world of work by preparing students for life after graduation….the Career Center offers services which include: career counseling; 3 classes for academic credit; workshops and seminars on career-related subjects; assistance with resume writing and interviewing; and opportunities for part-time jobs, internships, and full-time jobs.	2. Students will be aware of employment opportunities.	2a. Records maintained will indicate an increase of 5% in number of students attending job search workshops. 2b. On Alumni survey given one year after graduation, graduates will indicate a 3.4 agreement to question: "The Career Center increased my awareness of employment opportunities in my field of study."	2a. There was a 9% increase in the number of job search workshops presented and an increase of 17% in the number of students attending the workshops. 2b. Graduates on the Alumni Survey indicated a 3.3 agreement to question: "The Career Center increased my awareness of employment opportunities in my field of study."
	3. The number of opportunities for students to find employment will increase.	3a. Career Center records will indicate the number of resumes referred to employers will increase 24% over previous year. 3b. Career Center records will indicate the number of companies attending "Job Fairs" will increase 10% over previous year.	3a. Number of resumes forwarded to employers was 9% over last year. Major decrease was in resumes for business and accounting majors. 3b. The number of companies attending "Job Fairs" last year increased from 141 to 173. However, companies coming to campus for recruiting decreased 17%.

Figure 36

Accounting Office
Four-Column Model

Institutional Mission/ Goals Reference	Unit Mission Statement	Administrative Objectives	Means of Assessment & Criteria for Success	Summary of Data Collected

Institutional Mission/ Goals Reference

Goal 7.... the university will maintain efficient and effective administrative services to support the university's instructional, research, and public service programs.

Unit Mission Statement

The Accounting Office seeks (1) to provide administrators with accurate and timely financial data to assist them in the management of the institution's resources, and (2) to ensure that financial records are maintained in accordance with generally accepted accounting principles and guidelines as established by State and Federal agencies.

Administrative Objectives

1. Maintain financial systems in accordance with commonly accepted accounting practices.

2. Provide monthly financial reports by object of expenditure concerning expenditures and remaining balances to departments.

3. Process vendor statements for services promptly.

Means of Assessment & Criteria for Success

1. The University will receive an unqualified financial audit report each year.

2a. Monthly reports of expenditures and remaining balances by object of expenditure will be found to have been produced within the first three working days of the past twelve months.

2b. 90% of departmental heads/chairs who complete a two-hour workshop will "agree" or "strongly agree" with the survey item, "I understand and feel comfortable with the monthly financial statement."

3. An analysis of ten randomly-selected vendor statements monthly will reveal that no more than an average of five working days passed between receipt and payment. No statement will be found to have taken more than 10 days to process.

Summary of Data Collected

1. Audit report received within the last six months was unqualified.

2a. Monthly reports all found to have been produced and distributed promptly.

2b. 93% of workshop participants reported "understanding and being comfortable with financial reports"; however, attendance at workshops has sharply declined while complaints from heads/chairs have seemingly increased.

3. Average processing of vendor statements or invoices ranged from 6.5 to 7.2 days during the past twelve months. Two statements found to be delayed 14 and 17 days, respectively, due to lack of tax identification number.

Figure 37

Library
Four-Column Model

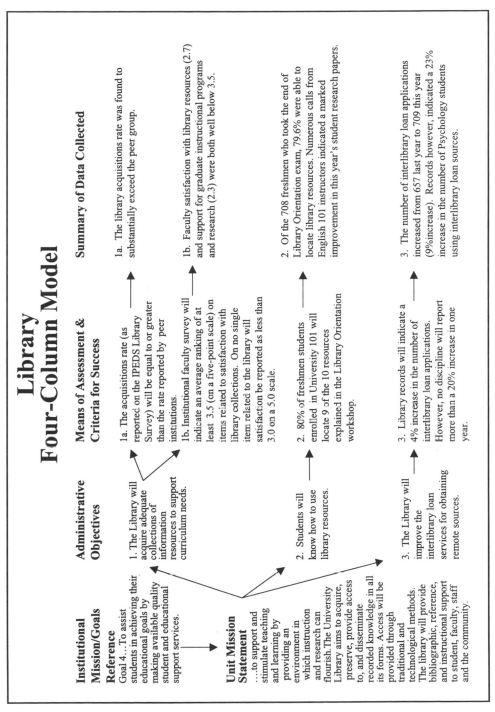

Institutional Mission/Goals Reference

Goal 4...To assist students in achieving their educational goals by making available quality student and educational support services.

Unit Mission Statement

....to support and stimulate teaching and learning by providing an environment in which instruction and research can flourish.The University Library aims to acquire, preserve, provide access to, and disseminate recorded knowledge in all its forms. Access will be provided through traditional and technological methods. The library will provide bibliographic, reference, and instructional support to student, faculty, staff and the community.

Administrative Objectives

1. The Library will acquire adequate collections of information resources to support curriculum needs.

2. Students will know how to use library resources.

3. The Library will improve the interlibrary loan services for obtaining remote sources.

Means of Assessment & Criteria for Success

1a. The acquisitions rate (as reported on the IPEDS Library Survey) will be equal to or greater than the rate reported by peer institutions.

1b. Institutional faculty survey will indicate an average ranking of at least 3.5 (on a five-point scale) on items related to satisfaction with library collections. On no single item related to the library will satisfaction be reported as less than 3.0 on a 5.0 scale.

2. 80% of freshmen students enrolled in University 101 will locate 9 of the 10 resources explained in the Library Orientation workshop.

3. Library records will indicate a 4% increase in the number of interlibrary loan applications. However, no discipline will report more than a 20% increase in one year.

Summary of Data Collected

1a. The library acquisitions rate was found to substantially exceed the peer group.

1b. Faculty satisfaction with library resources (2.7) and support for graduate instructional programs and research (2.3) were both well below 3.5.

2. Of the 708 freshmen who took the end of Library Orientation exam, 79.6% were able to locate library resources. Numerous calls from English 101 instructors indicated a marked improvement in this year's student research papers.

3. The number of interlibrary loan applications increased from 657 last year to 709 this year (9%increase). Records however, indicated a 23% increase in the number of Psychology students using interlibrary loan sources.

available from CQI/TQM are utilized *only* when a shortfall in expectations is encountered in an AES unit's assessment implementation, rather than broadly and comprehensively in all aspects of the unit in an independent CQI/TQM activity.

Creation of an Occasion to Use Assessment Results

The AES unit will need to *create an occasion* for review of assessment results. In many cases, simply incorporating assessment results into ongoing AES unit meetings will not provide an opportunity for discussions of the depth of consideration needed. Several campuses have used a half-day retreat during the summer months very successfully for this purpose. The AES department head, in conjunction with other staff, should prepare a summary of the data resulting from the assessment which has taken place. This summary should focus upon an application of the data to each administrative objective.

The data prepared should be distributed for review by the staff before an AES unit staff meeting is scheduled. Changes in AES unit services will come forward much more easily if the staff are involved in identifying the nature of the necessary changes. Likewise, staff should take part in celebrating the numerous instances in which assessment data clearly indicate their success. There cannot be too many occasions upon which AES staff are complimented for their achievements. On one campus the authors visited, each summer there would be a special staff meeting lasting several hours during which each AES unit would be asked to describe its major achievements and service improvements during the past year.

Types of Changes to Be Expected as a Result of Assessment Activities in AES Units

As a result of assessment activities, administrative and educational support (AES) units can anticipate changes in organizational structure, resource commitment patterns, administrative procedures, relationships to external agencies and the public, as well as the means of assessment and types of measures utilized to assess their services. While few administrative/educational support units will exhibit most of these types of changes, each unit should experience at least some of them.

Organizational Changes

Changes in AES unit organization, planning, reporting relationships, staff responsibilities and training are frequently cited as a result of assessment activities. Units often find that assessment results suggest the need to restructure the unit, as well as reporting responsibilities and supervisor relationships. This is frequently coupled with shifts or refinements in individual staff responsibilities in order to better accomplish the unit's administrative objectives. Once unit restructuring and realignment have taken place, training (and upon occasion cross-training) sessions are held to better acquaint employees with their assignments and the means for their accomplishment. Such administrative planning and reorganization lead naturally to the establishment of revised plans for AES unit operations that in many cases include shifting of unit priorities or emphasis to better achieve unit administrative objectives. This may be accompanied by deemphasis of some unit services in order to provide the resources necessary to achieve administrative objectives now seen as a priority by the AES unit.

Resource Reallocation

In some cases, internal resource reallocation takes place as a result of assessment activities. A number of AES units report shifting funds from one area to another in order to better accomplish their administrative objectives. As a result of client feedback, still other units have found it necessary to improve physical facilities in order to make them more attractive and functional. It is also not unusual to find unit realization that accomplishment of administrative objectives will be possible only through privately funded activities and to see these AES units initiate fund raising campaigns.

Changes in Procedures

As one might well imagine, assessment results frequently lead to changing unit procedures. A number of units make direct changes in the processes designed to provide the services assessed. This includes workshops or seminars offered by AES units. In a number of other instances, AES units have not changed their service delivery procedures, but improved the timeliness of the service delivery and thereby achieved increased client satisfaction.

Relations with the Public and Other Units

Assessment activities often lead to changes in the AES unit's relations with other units and the public. Frequently, AES units determine from client satisfaction measures that their unit primarily needs to improve its marketing of existing services, while other units have changed their name, added a logo and sought to completely change their "image" with their service constituency.

It is also not unusual to find AES units begin administrative planning by strengthening their relationship with other parties or units as a result of assessment activities. In some cases, this is accomplished by a conscious effort to improve liaison with other AES units and instructional programs, while in still other cases changes in AES unit procedures are made to better "fit" or "link" with other units. These units with which a better relationship is sought are frequently within the institution, but upon occasion, are agencies external to the campus.

Changes in Assessment Procedures

Particularly during the first iteration of assessment activities, AES units can expect to change their means for assessment and criteria for success. In many cases, AES units report substantial improvements/changes in record keeping and documentation as a result of assessment activities. Frequently, AES units increase their criteria for success after having become confident in their ability.

Changes to Comply with Regulatory Requirements

External evaluators representing regulatory agencies are likely to bring about changes in the manner in which AES units perform. When external evaluators compare current unit performance to "commonly accepted good practices of the field" and return adverse regulatory findings, the institution has little choice other than to change or face undesirable consequences.

Assessment Results as Justification For Additional Resources
Justification of the need for additional resources is a potential secondary use of assessment results. However, when faced with areas on our campuses needing improvement, in too many cases the first (and in some cases only) solution seen by AES unit heads is additional resources. As described earlier in Figure 3 (page 18), the use of assessment results by AES units as a basis for budget requests should be approached with great caution. In reality, many of the changes and improvements in services identified through assessment information can be brought about within existing resources. Before asking for additional resources as a result of assessment activities, the AES unit staff should thoroughly explore two questions. First, "Isn't there a means for improving our services without additional funding?" Second, "What are we going to do to improve services if additional funding is unavailable?"

The use of assessment results to improve unit services should be the ultimate intention of all assessment activity conducted by the AES unit. Whether that use is to change the nature of the services provided, the procedures used to provide the current services, the means of assessment, or potentially to inform the planning/ budgeting process, each AES unit must clearly identify how assessment results obtained have been substantively used.

Actions to Be Taken If the AES Unit Meets Its Criteria for Success

First, recognition of accomplishment should take place. In most cases, AES unit personnel will find that their efforts meet the criteria for success and that accomplishment should be visibly recognized within and without the unit. One potential way to accomplish this recognition is an annual institution-wide staff review of the use of assessment results during a scheduled meeting at the beginning of the year. During this review, staff can relate both occasions upon which they have met their criteria for success as well as improvements in services brought about as a result of assessment activities.

Though the criteria for success may have been met, AES unit staff are encouraged to conduct further analysis of the data to determine if additional information leading to other areas of service improvement are suggested. It is not uncommon to find changes in AES unit operations taking place based upon such secondary analysis of assessment data even though the unit has met their primary criteria for success. Be sure to give your unit credit for these changes by documenting such improvements while also reporting your meeting the criteria for success. An example of this is provided in the Accounting Office Five-Column Model (Figure 40) in "Use of Results" 2b and the Career Center Five-Column Model (Figure 39) in "Use of Results" 1a.

If the unit meets its criteria for success as measured by the assessment results received, the means of assessment should (in most cases) be monitored for several iterations to ensure continuation of successful operations. Then the administrative objective should be returned to the Long List and another brought forward for assessment. This procedure validates the Short List/Long List concept while demonstrating a systematic process of using assessment results to improve services. It also keeps the AES unit from attempting more assessment at any one time than it is capable of accomplishing.

Demonstration of the Use of Assessment Results to Improve Services in AES Units

Figures 38-41 depict the completed six steps and the Five-Column Models for the Office of the Registrar, the Career Center, Accounting Office and the Library which this publication has been tracing since Chapter Three. These Five-Column Models represent the completed assessment activities or "Closing of the Loop" within an educational support or administrative unit. Conceptually, they show the linkage between the components, highlight the assessment results and demonstrate how information collected from the means of assessment has lead to the improvement of services by AES units. These figures conceptually represent the standard toward which AES units should strive and should, as of the date of this publication, meet regional accreditation expectations in any region of the country.

While the Five-Column Models presented are conceptually complete and useful in explaining the process and procedures, they are not suggested or provided as a means through which to document an AES unit's achievements. While the Five-Column Model works well to explain the concept, experience has proven the model to "break down" in Columns 4 and 5 when AES units attempt to record actual results and their use in the small space available. The chapter which follows and the forms provided retain the concepts shown in the Five-Column Model (including the linkage between the components), but shift them from landscape into a portrait format on forms which can be easily downloaded from the Internet website: *www.iea-nich.com.*

Figure 38

Office of the Registrar Five-Column Model

Institutional Mission/Goals Reference	Unit Mission Statement	Administrative Objectives	Means of Assessment & Criteria for Success	Summary of Data Collected	Use of Results
Goal #4: To assist students in achieving their educational goals by making available quality student and educational support services.	The Registrar's Office is responsible for processing applications for admission, processing and reporting student enrollment, maintaining registered student records, receiving grades, and the processing of transcript information.	1. Increase student satisfaction with the overall registration process.	1a. Responses on the Graduating Student Survey related to "overall satisfaction with the registration process" will average from 2.7 to 3.5 on a five-point scale. 1b. The number of "complaints" left in the Registrar's "suggestion box" will decrease from an average of 53 each semester to approximately 40. No single area of service will receive more than 1/3 of the suggestions each month.	1a. Response improved to 3.2; however, response of students attending after 7:00 p.m. remained unchanged at 1.9. 1b. The number of "complaints" increased to an average of 55. Many of these complaints related to computer response time.	1a. Progress noted. Office of the Registrar to remain open until 8:00 p.m. during registration and for first week of class by re-scheduling of employees. 1b. Installation of new hardware should reduce comments next semester.
		2. Shorten response time for transcript requests.	2a. The average number of days from receipt of transcript requests to posting of response will be reduced from 4.5 to 3.5 days based upon a one week sample taken at random each semester. No transcript request will be found to have longer than five working days. 2b. "Over the counter" requests for transcripts will be filled within 24 hours as measured one day each month.	2a. Average response time for mail requests was 3.3 days during proceeding twelve months. Longest response time found to be 4 1/2 days. 2b. During registration and pre-registration, many "over the counter requests" were unfilled after 48 hours.	2a. Staff voted to monitor one more year. Records are being kept regarding high demand time for possible shift in personnel. 2b. Staff diversion from transcript request service during registration no longer authorized.
		3. Provide accurate class enrollment data.	3a. Student credit hour auditors from the governing board will verify the accuracy of class enrollments each semester reporting "no adjustments required."	3a. In most recent two audits, class enrollment reporting was verified and "no adjustments required."	3a. Due to importance to institutional formula funding, continue to be monitored.

Figure 39

Career Center
Five-Column Model

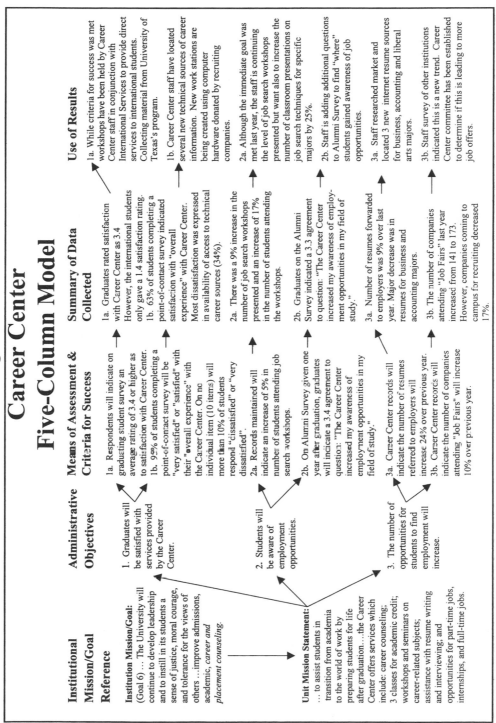

Institutional Mission/Goal Reference	Administrative Objectives	Means of Assessment & Criteria for Success	Summary of Data Collected	Use of Results
Institution Mission/Goal: (Goal 6) ... The University will continue to develop leadership and to instill in its students a sense of justice, moral courage, and tolerance for the views of others ...improve admissions, academic, *career and placement counseling.*	1. Graduates will be satisfied with services provided by the Career Center.	1a. Respondents will indicate on graduating student survey an average rating of 3.4 or higher as to satisfaction with Career Center. 1b. 95% of students completing a point-of-contact survey will be "very satisfied" or "satisfied" with their "overall experience" with the Career Center. On no individual item (10 items) will more than 10% of students respond "dissatisfied" or "very dissatisfied".	1a. Graduates rated satisfaction with Career Center as 3.4. However, the international students only gave a 1.4 satisfaction rating. 1b. 63% of students completing a point-of-contact survey indicated satisfaction with "overall experience" with Career Center. Most dissatisfaction was expressed in availability of access to technical career sources (34%).	1a. While criteria for success was met workshops have been held by Career Center staff in conjunction with International Services to provide direct services to international students. Collecting material from University of Texas's program. 1b. Career Center staff have located several new technical sources of career information. New work stations are being created using computer hardware donated by recruiting companies.
Unit Mission Statement: ... to assist students in transition from academia to the world of work by preparing students for life after graduation....the Career Center offers services which include: career counseling; 3 classes for academic credit; workshops and seminars on career-related subjects; assistance with resume writing and interviewing; and opportunities for part-time jobs, internships, and full-time jobs.	2. Students will be aware of employment opportunities.	2a. Records maintained will indicate an increase of 5% in number of students attending job search workshops. 2b. On Alumni Survey given one year after graduation, graduates will indicate a 3.4 agreement to question: "The Career Center increased my awareness of employment opportunities in my field of study."	2a. There was a 9% increase in the number of job search workshops presented and an increase of 17% in the number of students attending the workshops. 2b. Graduates on the Alumni Survey indicated a 3.3 agreement to question: "The Career Center increased my awareness of employment opportunities in my field of study."	2a. Although the immediate goal was met last year, the staff is continuing the level of job search workshops presented but want also to increase the number of classroom presentations on job search techniques for specific majors by 25%. 2b. Staff is adding additional questions to Alumni Survey to find "where" students gained awareness of job opportunities.
	3. The number of opportunities for students to find employment will increase.	3a. Career Center records will indicate the number of resumes referred to employers will increase 24% over previous year. 3b. Career Center records will indicate the number of companies attending "Job Fairs" will increase 10% over previous year.	3a. Number of resumes forwarded to employers was 9% over last year. Major decrease was in resumes for business and accounting majors. 3b. The number of companies attending "Job Fairs" last year increased from 141 to 173. However, companies coming to campus for recruiting decreased 17%.	3a. Staff researched market and located 3 new internet resume sources for business, accounting and liberal arts majors. 3b. Staff survey of other institutions indicated this is a new trend. Career Center committee has been established to determine if this is leading to more job offers.

Figure 40

Accounting Office
Five-Column Model

Institutional Mission/Goals Reference	Administrative Objectives	Means of Assessment and Criteria for Success	Summary of Data Collected	Use of Results
Goal 7.... the university will maintain efficient and effective administrative services to support the university's instructional, research, and public service programs.	1. Maintain financial systems in accordance with commonly accepted accounting practices.	1. The University will receive an unqualified financial audit report each year.	1. Audit report received within the last six months was unqualified.	1. Evaluate an additional year for consistency. Committee formed to identify other accounting aspects to assess for service improvements.
Unit Mission Statement	2. Provide monthly financial reports by object of expenditure concerning expenditures and remaining balances to departments.	2a. Monthly reports of expenditures and remaining balances by object of expenditure will be found to have been produced within the first three working days of the past twelve months.	2a. Monthly reports all found to have been produced and distributed promptly.	2a. Process is being evaluated by internal auditor in more detail to determine how much overtime the process is taking.
The Accounting Office seeks (1) to provide administrators with accurate and timely financial data to assist them in the management of the institution's resources, and (2) to ensure that financial records are maintained in accordance with generally accepted accounting principles and guidelines as established by State and Federal agencies.		2b. 90% of departmental heads/chairs who complete a two-hour workshop will "agree" or "strongly agree" with the survey item, "I understand and feel comfortable with the monthly financial statement."	2b. 93% of workshop participants reported "understanding and being comfortable with financial reports"; however, attendance at workshops has sharply declined while complaints from heads/chairs have seemingly increased.	2b. While the criteria for success was met, workshops are being offered four times annually and deans have agreed to require department heads/chairs to attend one of the four workshops yearly.
	3. Process vendor statements for services promptly.	3. An analysis of ten randomly-selected vendor statements monthly will reveal that no more than an average of five working days passed between receipt and payment. No statement will be found to have taken more than 10 days to process.	3. Average processing of vendor statements or invoices ranged from 6.5 to 7.2 days during the past twelve months. Two statements found to be delayed 14 and 17 days, respectively, due to lack of tax identification number.	3. Staff has indicated that this is a real problem. They submitted suggestions and staff workshops were held to improve efficiency. Vendors not providing tax identification number are now called within 24 hours of receipt of their statement.

Figure 41

Library
Five-Column Model

Institutional Mission/Goals Reference	Administrative Objectives	Means of Assessment & Criteria for Success	Summary of Data Collected	Use of Results
Goal 4...To assist students in achieving their educational goals by making available quality student and educational support services.	1. The Library will acquire adequate collections of information resources to support curriculum needs.	1a. The acquisitions rate (as reported on the IPEDS Library Survey) will be equal to or greater than the rate reported by peer institutions.	1a. The library acquisitions rate was found to substantially exceed the peer group.	1a. No actions required at this time. Monitor closely due to current impact of private gifts on library acquisitions.
Unit Mission Statement		1 b. Institutional faculty survey will indicate an average ranking of at least 3.5 (on a five-point scale) on items related to satisfaction with library collections. On no single item related to the library will satisfaction be reported as less than 3.0 on a 5.0 scale.	1b. Faculty satisfaction with library resources (2.7) and support for graduate instructional programs and research (2.3) were both well below 3.5.	1b. Acquisitions in coming year shifted to better service graduate programs and research. Focus groups formed to elicit more specific reason for dissatisfaction. Original survey results being sorted by school/college to gain better focus on perceived inadequacies.
....to support and stimulate teaching and learning by providing an environment in which instruction and research can flourish.The University Library aims to acquire, preserve, provide access to, and disseminate recorded knowledge in all its forms. Access will be provided through traditional and technological methods. The library will provide bibliographic, reference, and instructional support to students, faculty, staff and the community.	2. Students will know how to use library resources.	2. 80% of freshmen students enrolled in University 101 will locate 9 of the 10 resources explained in the Library Orientation workshop.	2. Of the 708 freshmen who took the end of Library Orientation exam, 79.6% were able to locate library resources. Numerous calls from English 101 instructors indicated a marked improvement in this year's student research papers.	2. Developed a similar Library Orientation program on a monthly basis for all students.
	3. The Library will improve the interlibrary loan services for obtaining remote sources.	3. Library records will indicate a 4% increase in the number of interlibrary loan applications. However, no discipline will report more than a 20% increase in one year.	3. The number of interlibrary loan applications increased from 657 last year to 709 this year (9%increase). Records however, indicated a 23% increase in the number of Psychology students using interlibrary loan sources.	3. Committee of library staff and Psychology faculty has been established to review library holdings in Psychology.

CHAPTER V

DOCUMENTATION OF ASSESSMENT ACTIVITIES AND USE OF RESULTS TO IMPROVE SERVICES BY ADMINISTRATIVE AND EDUCATIONAL SUPPORT UNITS

The end result of the assessment activities described previously is the improvement of unit services as reflected by a documented and systematic process whereby assessment activities have led to service improvements in educational support and administrative units. The key concept discussed in this chapter is *documentation* of that systematic process to use assessment results in making service improvements.

It is absolutely necessary to create at least a minimal, but consistent, "paper trail" for describing assessment activities throughout the campus and the resulting program improvements. According to one of the regional accrediting association employees in the Fall Semester 1998, "If it isn't written down, it didn't happen." This is necessary because so many institutions have promised implementation of assessment activities leading to service improvements and then failed to fulfill those promises. In many ways, the situation between institutions and their regional accrediting associations is similar to that in arms reduction negotiations between President Ronald Reagan and Mr. Mikhail Gorbachev representing the former Soviet Union. In those negotiations, President Reagan said that he would "Trust, but verify." Regional accrediting associations' representatives will trust, but verify through review of your documentation that assessment has taken place and service improvements thereby have been brought about.

The information presented should be concise and focused, relating in a systematic manner administrative objectives, assessment results, and reports of verifiable actions to improve services. There is no requirement that a "dissertation or thesis" be prepared regarding assessment activities in an AES unit. There needs to be enough information within the report to clearly show the systematic nature of the assessment procedure, convince the reader that the assessment activities actually took place, and describe the nature of the changes in unit operations which resulted from the assessment activities which took place.

Responsibility for this documentation of assessment activities normally lies with the AES unit department head. At that level, there should be clear awareness of how the AES assessment plan was implemented, the assessment results, and how the data were used to improve services. There also needs to be a consistent set of documentation describing such activities across the institution. Members of the institution's reaffirmation visitation committee should not be challenged to find examples of implementation in multiple types of assessment report styles or formats used across the institution. For the most part, they will not have the time to accept such a challenge and the institution will be the losers and find itself writing reports or preparing for further visits. There should be one simple, readable, consistent and understandable means for documentation of assessment processes and use of results which visiting team members can readily identify from unit to unit.

One of the challenges faced in administrative and educational support units is maintaining records of any type over a considerable period of time. *The single most evident factor in discontinuance of assessment implementation within an AES unit is a change in unit leadership.* Countless times the authors have encountered circumstances in which the previous AES department head had led a successful implementation of assessment activities, but (in the transition to the current unit leader) passing on that assessment initiative and experience has "fallen through the cracks." Likewise, one of the greatest problems in maintenance of assessment documentation is encountered in the change of departmental clerical or secretarial personnel. It is these personnel who in many cases actually maintain the documentation. At the authors' institution, workshops are held each fall semester for new department heads and chairs to make them aware of their responsibilities for assessment leadership. Separate workshops are conducted for departmental unit clerical personnel in maintaining assessment documentation. The Assessment Record Book described in the balance of this section, will fulfill the need of the institution to maintain summary type assessment documentation for as long as eight to ten years in order to provide the paper trail necessary to meet regional accreditation expectations. At the same time, the concise information and format allows the institution to clearly show evidence of a systematic process to meet regional accreditation expectations.

The Assessment Record Book concept and forms described in this chapter (see Figures 42-46) are recommended as one relatively simple and straightforward way to accomplish the necessary assessment documentation. These forms are maintained at the AES unit level and enjoy the following advantages:

- They retain the linkages in the Five-Column Model previously explained.
- They highlight the systematic nature of the assessment process by leading from the Expanded Statement of Institutional Purpose to the Unit Mission Statement, to the unit administrative objectives, means of assessment, assessment results, and use of results.
- They are tightly focused to provide the minimum documentation necessary.
- They may be downloaded from the Internet from the Institutional Effectiveness Associates' (IEA) web site (*www.iea-nich.com*) at no cost.

Figure 42

Transition Five-Column Model to Assessment Record

Career Center

ASSESSMENT REPORT

FOR

_____
(Administrative or Educational Support Unit)

_____   _____
(Assessment Period Covered)   (Date Submitted)

COLUMN 1

Institutional Mission/Goals Reference

Goal 6... The University will continue to develop leadership and to instill in its students a sense of..........career and placement counseling

Extended Statement of Institutional Purpose Linkage:

Institutional Mission/Goal(s) Reference:

Administrative or Educational Support Unit Mission Statement:

Unit Mission Statement:

...to assist students in transition from academia to the world of work by preparing students for life after graduation....the Career Center offers services which include: career counseling; 3 classes for academic credit; workshops and seminars on career-related subjects; assistance.....

Intended Administrative Objectives:

1.

2.

3.

Form B

Figure 43

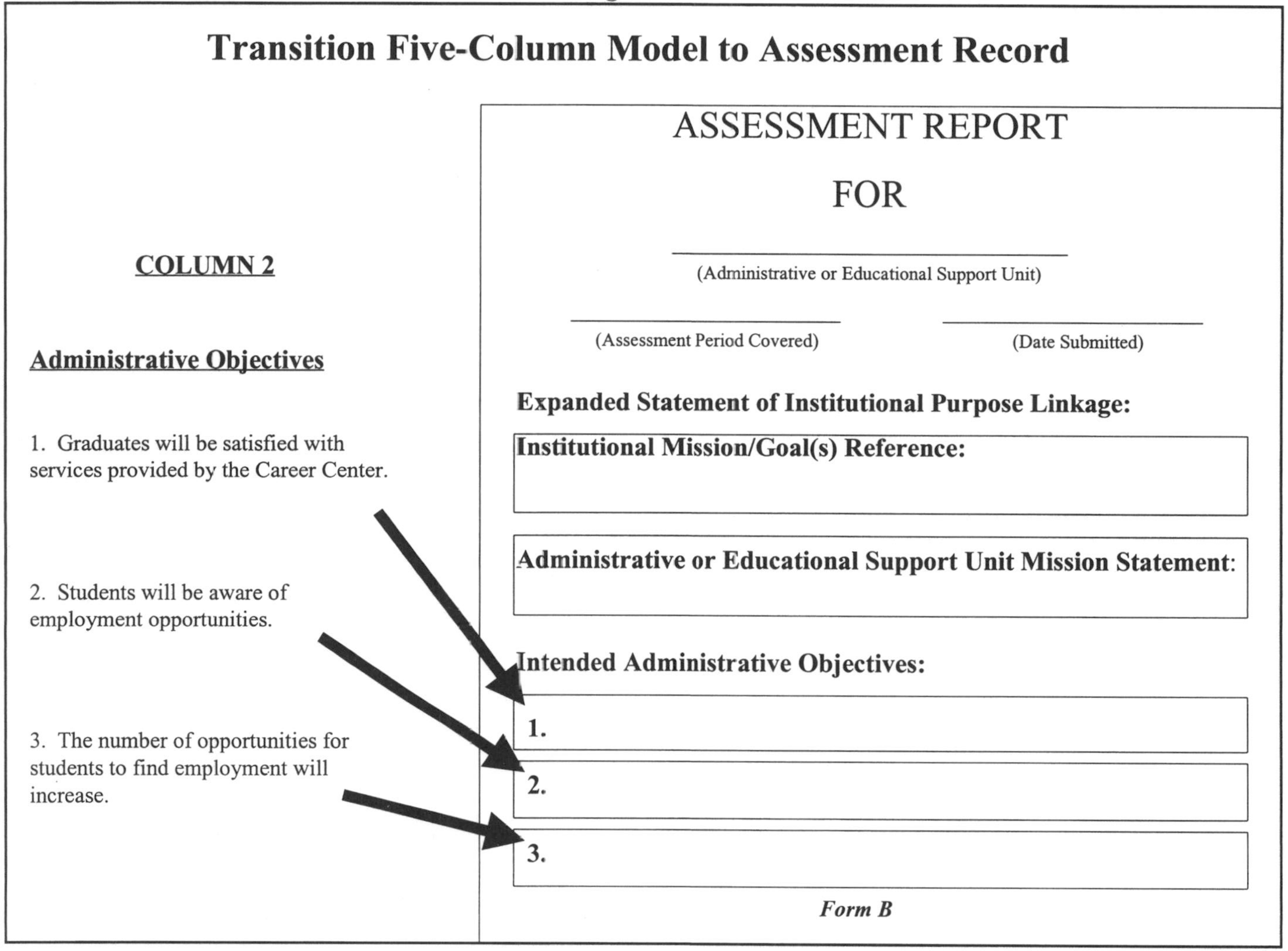

Transition Five-Column Model to Assessment Record

ASSESSMENT REPORT

FOR

_____
(Administrative or Educational Support Unit)

_____   _____
(Assessment Period Covered)   (Date Submitted)

Expanded Statement of Institutional Purpose Linkage:

Institutional Mission/Goal(s) Reference:

Administrative or Educational Support Unit Mission Statement:

Intended Administrative Objectives:

1.

2.

3.

Form B

COLUMN 2

Administrative Objectives

1. Graduates will be satisfied with services provided by the Career Center.

2. Students will be aware of employment opportunities.

3. The number of opportunities for students to find employment will increase.

Figure 44

Transition Five-Column Model to Assessment Record

ASSESSMENT REPORT

FOR

_____
(Administrative or Educational Support Unit)

_____   _____
(Assessment Period Covered)   (Date Submitted)

Intended Administrative or Educational Support Objective:

NOTE: There should be one Form C for each administrative objective listed on Form B. Administrative unit objective should be restated in the box immediately below and the administrative objective number entered in the blank spaces.

1.

First Means of Assessment for Objective Identified Above:

1a. Means of Unit Assessment & Criteria for Success:

1a. Summary of Assessment Data Collected:

1a. Use of Results to Improve Unit Services:

Second Means of Assessment for Objective Identified Above:

1b. Means of Unit Assessment & Criteria for Success:

1b. Summary of Assessment Data Collected:

1b. Use of Results to Improve Unit Services:

Form C

COLUMN 2

Administrative Objectives:

1. Graduates will be satisfied with services provided by the Career Center.

COLUMN 3

Means of Assessment & Criteria for Success:

1a. Respondents will indicate on graduating student survey an average rating of 3.4 or higher as to satisfaction with Career Center.

1b. 95% of students completing a point-of-contact survey will be "very satisfied" or "satisfied" with their "overall experience" with the Career Center. On no individual item (10 items) will more than 10% of students respond "dissatisfied" or "very dissatisfied".

2a.

2b.

3a.

3b.

Figure 45

Transition Five-Column Model to Assessment Record

ASSESSMENT REPORT

FOR

_____
(Administrative or Educational Support Unit)

_____   _____
(Assessment Period Covered)   (Date Submitted)

Intended Administrative or Educational Support Objective:

NOTE: There should be one Form C for each administrative objective listed on Form B. Administrative unit objective should be restated in the box immediately below and the Administrative objective number entered in the blank spaces.

1. [   ]

First Means of Assessment for Objective Identified Above:

1a. Means of Unit Assessment & Criteria for Success: [   ]

1a. Summary of Assessment Data Collected: [   ]

1a. Use of Results to Improve Unit Services: [   ]

Second Means of Assessment for Objective Identified Above:

b. Means of Unit Assessment & Criteria for Success: [   ]

1b. Summary of Assessment Data Collected: [   ]

1b. Use of Results to Improve Unit Services: [   ]

Form C

COLUMN 4

Summary of Assessment Data Collected:

1a. Graduates rated satisfaction with Career Center as 3.4. However, the international students only gave a 1.4 satisfaction rating.

1b. 63% of students completing a point-of-contact survey indicated satisfaction with "overall experience" with Career Center. Most dissatisfaction was expressed in availability of access to technical career sources (34%).

2a.

2b.

3a.

3b.

Figure 46

Transition Five-Column Model to Assessment Record

ASSESSMENT REPORT

FOR

_____
(Administrative or Educational Support Unit)

_____ _____
(Assessment Period Covered) (Date Submitted)

Intended Administrative or Educational Support Objective:

NOTE: There should be one Form C for each administrative objective listed on Form B. Administrative unit objective should be restated in the box immediately below and the Administrative objective number entered in the blank spaces.

1.

First Means of Assessment for Objective Identified Above:

1a. Means of Unit Assessment & Criteria for Success:

1a. Summary of Assessment Data Collected:

1a. Use of Results to Improve Unit Services:

Second Means of Assessment for Objective Identified Above:

1b. Means of Unit Assessment & Criteria for Success:

1b. Summary of Assessment Data Collected:

1b. Use of Results to Improve Unit Services:

Form C

COLUMN 5

Use of Results to Improve Unit Services:

1a While criteria for success were met, workshops have been held by Career Center staff in conjunction with International Services to provide direct services to international students. Collecting material from University of Texas' program.

1b Career Center staff have located several new technical sources of career information. New work stations are being created using computer hardware donated by recruiting companies.

2a.

2b.

3a.

3b.

The Assessment Record Book consists of three types of forms—Forms A, B, and C provided in Appendix A. Form A constitutes little more than a cover sheet. Form B links the AES unit through its Unit Mission Statement to the Expanded Statement of Purpose and lists the administrative objectives for the unit during the assessment period (covering columns one and two of the Five-Column Model, see Figures 42 and 43). Form C constitutes an assessment report concerning each administrative objective; its means of assessment and criteria for success (see Figure 44); a summary of the assessment data (see Figure 45); and a description of how this assessment was utilized to improve services (see Figure 46). Completion of these forms requires AES units to move from planning to implementation and "Closing the Loop." In most cases, annual documentation of assessment activities through the Assessment Record Book forms can be accomplished by AES units in approximately five word-processed pages each year. These annual reports should be accumulated as depicted in Figure 47 so that an historical record of assessment activities is available at the time of the accreditation reaffirmation visitation.

Figure 47

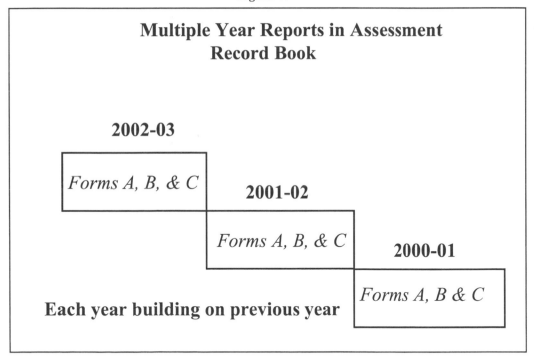

Appendix A contains copies of Form A, B, and C, as well as an example of their completion utilizing the Career Center Five-Column Model previously shown in Figure 39. It must be noted that these example pages have been reduced in size from the 8 ½ x 11 inch standard format which should be utilized in the unit's Assessment Record Book.

These forms, as well as instructions for completing them, are available for downloading from the IEA web site at *www.iea-nich.com*. They can be downloaded directly into either Microsoft Word® or WordPerfect® software existing on your campus.

Each institution should keep two copies of the Assessment Record Book for each administrative or educational support unit. One copy should be maintained at the unit level and provides documentation readily accessible to unit staff. The other copy should be housed at the institutional level by the party responsible for seeing that assessment takes place on the campus. This second copy can be used to monitor the completion of Assessment Record Book forms and may be made readily available to accreditation reaffirmation visiting team members to fulfill the need for institution-wide evidence of implementation cited earlier in this chapter. It also serves as a backup copy when unit Assessment Record Books are lost or misplaced during personnel transitions.

Whatever means of documentation is selected by an institution, it needs to be consistently maintained throughout all AES units. The Assessment Record Book procedure explained in this chapter and depicted in Appendix A is a relatively easy way to maintain this necessary documentation consistently across the institution without "reinventing the wheel."

CHAPTER VI

ASSESSMENT IN ORGANIZED RESEARCH AND EXTERNAL SERVICE/ CONTINUING EDUCATION UNITS

Assessment in Organized Research Units

The requirement to assess the effectiveness of organized research activities is present in most regional accrediting association requirements. Exemplary of these requirements is that from the Commission on Colleges, Southern Association of Colleges and Schools which states that "The institution must develop guidelines and procedures to evaluate educational effectiveness, including the quality of student learning, and of research and service."

"Organized" research is different and separate from less structured research conducted by individual department faculty in several ways. First, it is normally conducted by a group of faculty working cooperatively in a specific field for a prolonged period of time. Second, it is frequently funded separately by the institution or through external grants and contracts. Finally, organized research activities are most often housed within separate organizational units identified as centers, institutes, etc. These AES organizational units are free-standing, reporting to the department or the academic dean responsible, or upon occasion, directly to the institutional level.

Organized research units spring from a number of different sources. Frequently, institutions will seek to combine the research activities taking place within a number of departments into a more general field creating a more visible research entity such as a "Center for Social Science Research," which combines the research activities previously pursued separately by individual faculty in history, government, economics, political science, etc. This action often takes place in an effort to attract more external grants to fund the research conducted. On other occasions, faculty in a given discipline will identify a major research component of their field or discipline within which to establish a center such as physical acoustics, wireless communication, etc. for research in depth. Finally, upon occasion, an individual faculty member's research grant may grow to the point that it takes on a "life of its own" with a complete support structure, as well as separate budgetary and organizational status at an institution.

There are a number of common measures of assessment in organized research units. These include: the number of grant proposals submitted, the number of grant proposals funded, the amount of external funding received, and the professional recognition of faculty and staff housed in the organized research unit. Note that none of these means of assessment deal directly with the results of the research conducted. All are "process oriented" means of assessment which are assumed to indirectly reflect upon the quality of the research being conducted.

The "number of grant proposals submitted" is frequently cited as a means of assessment for institutional level units charged with overall coordination of organized research at an institution. This measure is utilized as an indicator of the overall success of the unit (office) in stimulating the institution's faculty to submit proposals for organized research activities. It is most commonly found when one combined institutional level organized research assessment plan is developed.

The "number of grant proposals funded" is also a common means of assessment utilized by organized research units as well as those units charged with overall coordination of research at the institutional level. Unlike the number of grant proposals submitted, this means of assessment does exhibit an indirect qualitative reflection of the nature of the research proposals prepared. In the peer review process, many grant proposals are reviewed by a panel or jury of experts in the field working for the funding agency. It is assumed that the relative merit of the grant proposals considered will be determined by these external evaluators by (a) the nature of the current proposal and (b) the reputation of the organized research unit submitting the proposal.

Combining the two means of assessment referenced previously (grant proposals submitted and grant proposals funded), it is possible to calculate a ratio of proposals funded to proposals submitted which can be utilized as an index of the effectiveness of the proposal preparation process.

The "amount of external funding received" is also frequently found as a means of assessment for organized research. The operative assumption in this regard is that more expensive research is better research. While that assumption may or may not be valid, more expensive research is normally associated with greater institutional return of indirect cost and is, therefore, valued on many campuses.

Finally, professional recognition of faculty and staff associated with organized research programs is occasionally utilized as a measure of research effectiveness. The means of professional recognition frequently cited are: (a) memberships in honorary orders or groups within professional organizations, (b) the number of faculty research presentations made at professional meetings; (c) the number of research papers accepted for publication; and (d) the selection of organized research faculty to serve on national panels which review research proposals submitted by peers.

As indicated above, none of these measures truly evaluate the nature of the research conducted; rather, they focus on the processes surrounding organized research activities. Figures 48 and 49 are provided to illustrate two approaches to assessment of organized research activities at institutions. Figure 48 depicts an organized research unit (such as the Office of University Research) at an institution which is charged with coordinating the overall organized research program at an

Figure 48

University Office of Research Five-Column Model

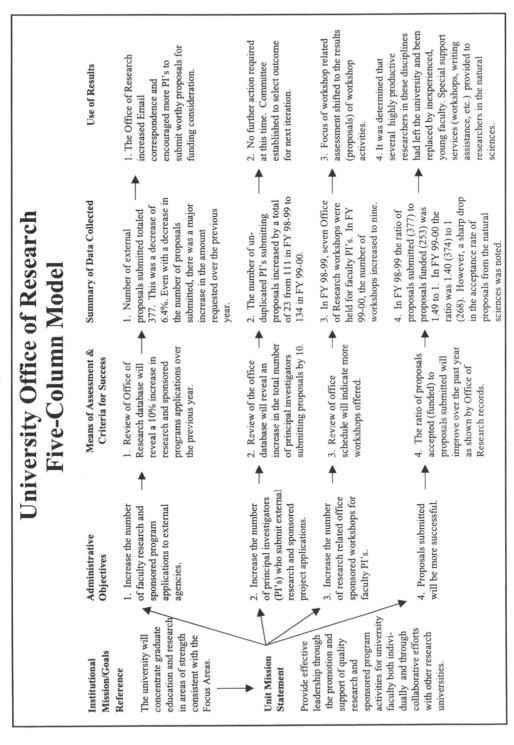

Institutional Mission/Goals Reference	Administrative Objectives	Means of Assessment & Criteria for Success	Summary of Data Collected	Use of Results
The university will concentrate graduate education and research in areas of strength consistent with the Focus Areas.	1. Increase the number of faculty research and sponsored program applications to external agencies.	1. Review of Office of Research database will reveal a 10% increase in research and sponsored programs applications over the previous year.	1. Number of external proposals submitted totaled 377. This was a decrease of 6.4%. Even with a decrease in the number of proposals submitted, there was a major increase in the amount requested over the previous year.	1. The Office of Research increased Email correspondence and encouraged more PI's to submit worthy proposals for funding consideration.
Unit Mission Statement Provide effective leadership through the promotion and support of quality research and sponsored program activities for university faculty both individually and through collaborative efforts with other research universities.	2. Increase the number of principal investigators (PI's) who submit external research and sponsored project applications.	2. Review of the office database will reveal an increase in the total number of principal investigators submitting proposals by 10.	2. The number of un-duplicated PI's submitting proposals increased by a total of 23 from 111 in FY 98-99 to 134 in FY 99-00.	2. No further action required at this time. Committee established to select outcome for next iteration.
	3. Increase the number of research related office sponsored workshops for faculty PI's.	3. Review of office schedule will indicate more workshops offered.	3. In FY 98-99, seven Office of Research workshops were held for faculty PI's. In FY 99-00, the number of workshops increased to nine.	3. Focus of workshop related assessment shifted to the results (proposals) of workshop activities.
	4. Proposals submitted will be more successful.	4. The ratio of proposals accepted (funded) to proposals submitted will improve over the past year as shown by Office of Research records.	4. In FY 98-99 the ratio of proposals submitted (377) to proposals funded (253) was 1.49 to 1. In FY 99-00 the ratio was 1.40 (374) to 1 (268). However, a sharp drop in the acceptance rate of proposals from the natural sciences was noted.	4. It was determined that several highly productive researchers in these disciplines had left the university and been replaced by inexperienced, young faculty. Special support services (workshops, writing assistance, etc.) provided to researchers in the natural sciences.

Figure 49

Coastal Fisheries Research Institute
Five-Column Model

Institutional Mission/Goals Reference	Administrative Objectives	Means of Assessment & Criteria for Success	Summary of Data Collected	Use of Results
The university will concentrate graduate education and research in areas of strength consistent with the Focus Areas.	1. The number and amount of external research grants concerning Coastal Fisheries will increase.	1. File copies and acceptance notices received and held in the Institute will record an increase each year.	1. The amount of funding received increased from \$3,727,939 to \$4,358,621; however, the number of grant proposals declined from 17 to 15.	1. Since funding increased sharply, the modest decline in number of proposals is not seen as justifying action at this time. Continue to monitor due to importance.
Unit Mission Statement The Coastal Fisheries Research Institute will conduct research, provide information, and establish collaborative relationships with industry which enhance the economic development of the coastal areas of the state.	2. Forecast of changes in Coastal Fisheries will be produced, disseminated, and utilized to set policy.	2a. Institute files will contain updated fisheries forecasts as well as mailing lists to whom they were forwarded. 2b. At least one specific industry or governmental policy influenced by fisheries forecast will be cited each year.	2a. Updated forecasts were found to be present as well as copies of mailing lists to whom they had been forwarded. 2b. As a result of the institute forecast, the allowable catch of red sea bass in the waters bordering the southern two counties in the state has been reduced by two-thirds.	2a. Since criteria was met, another administrative objective is being considered for next reporting cycle. 2b. Criteria for success to require both governmental and industry utilization in next cycle.
	3. New fishing industry companies will locate in our state each year to replace those individually owned boats being retired.	3. Information received from state Economic Development Agency (EDA) will confirm, at a minimum, maintenance of the number of active fishing boats.	3. Information received from EDA indicates four commercial companies (73 boats) relocated to coastal cities as result of favorable fisheries forecasts. These more than replaced the 57 individual boats that were taken from service.	3. Criteria met, however have developed a survey for new companies to determine what factors contributed to their location in the state.

institution. Figure 49, on the other hand, is a Five-Column Model specifically regarding a single major organized research center at an institution. Either approach is entirely acceptable as a means through which to meet regional accrediting association requirements.

Assessment in External Service/Continuing Education Units

Assessment in service units relates to measuring the effectiveness of units specifically organized for the provision of service (as opposed to credit bearing instruction hosted on the home campus) to clientele. It does not relate to the individual services provided on an ad hoc basis by faculty or staff throughout the institution. The definition of a "service unit" is among the more vexing in higher education. To restrict the definition of "service" units to that of "public service" units would exclude large numbers of services provided to the citizens through units such as continuing education, which is categorized for accounting purposes as "Community Instruction." On the other hand, the term service unit could be extended to include units such as the Library, Career Center, etc., which offers services primarily to students on the campus. For the sake of this chapter, the term "External Service Units" will be utilized to describe those units on any campus whose primary (but not exclusive) purpose is the provision of service (to include continuing education conducted at off-campus locations) to clients other than the students enrolled at the institution's main campus.

Among the types of external service units referenced are those found in continuing education, service centers, and extension education. Continuing education, non-credit programs, focused upon the provision of continuing professional education such as that required for pharmacists, accountants, bankers, etc., clearly fall under this definition. Additionally, service activities related to summer camps for athletics, cheerleading, drama, elder hostile, photography, and other subjects of personal interest to the participants are clearly included within this definition.

Separately organized external service units also exist on many campuses to provide focused services in a given specialty. Examples of these include hearing clinics, dental clinics, and other health related entities providing direct service to the public. The fact that these services are often provided by supervised students enrolled in institutional degree programs does not detract from their inclusion within our definition of external service units. In addition to health related external service units, services such as those related to small business development, population demographics and others are frequently found on campuses. Without any doubt, the largest external service agency in any state is housed at the state land grant university in the form of the extension services offered to a variety of clients in counties across the state.

The predominant means of assessment regarding external service units are client satisfaction and direct measures. Overall measures of client satisfaction with agencies such as university extension services are not uncommon. These surveys seek to identify the extent of overall client acceptance of the services provided. Even more common are point-of-contact client satisfaction measures that are typically provided at the time the client receives the treatment or services. Typical of these types of measures are surveys conducted following service regarding medical procedures or small business administration services.

Client satisfaction with instructional services received is a common form of assessment for non-credit educational programs provided to clients other than the institution's students. While this form of assessment would be considered inappropriate regarding the institution's instructional programs, because it is a measure of the educational process as opposed to its outcomes, it is an entirely appropriate means of assessment for the specialized external service units which are categorized as educational support in nature.

Direct measures or counts of services are also frequently employed as measures of effectiveness by external service units. These direct measures include:

- Number of patients served
- Number of program participants
- Variety of types of programming provided
- Geographic dispersion of services

In most cases, these data are already available within the external service unit and need only be tabulated for their utilization in assessment activities.

Included in Figure 50 is an example of completed assessment activities regarding a typical continuing education unit. Figure 51 provides an example of assessment activities within a unit specifically organized to provide direct external services.

Assessment activities regarding external service units are for the most part uncomplicated, in many cases already taking place, and easily documented. The requirement to demonstrate improvement in these services through assessment activities will grow steadily in the forthcoming years.

Figure 50

Continuing Education
Five-Column Model

Institutional Mission/Goals Reference	Administrative Objectives	Means of Assessment & Criteria for Success	Summary of Data Collected	Use of Results
The university will disseminate its expertise and knowledge to non-academic communities throughout the state of Mississippi and the Mid-South region.	1. Course offerings at off-campus locations will grow each year.	1. The total number of course sections offered at locations other than the main campus will increase 3%.	1. 121 courses offered off-campus this year compared to 107 last year. 13% increase.	1. Information used to guide continued expansion of class offering.
Unit Mission Statement .... Increase off-campus enrollments and offerings while expanding distance learning through electronic means.	2. Enrollment in off-campus courses will show a steady increase of students pleased with the instructional services provided.	2a. Total enrollment in off-campus courses will grow at least 4% per year. No discipline will record a decline of more than 15% in enrollment.	2a. Total course enrollment in off-campus courses is 1307 compared to 1276 last year; an increase of 2.4%. Business classes recorded biggest gain while math class enrollment dropped significantly (21%).	2a. Further study by faculty committee to determine preference for off-campus classes. Low attendance in math classes attributable to times specific math classes offered, schedule changed for this year.
		2b. Student responses to off-campus course evaluation to the item "I am satisfied with the instructional program offered at this location" will average 3.5 on a 5.0 scale for each location.	2b. Survey response averages were as follows by location: South Campus - 4.1; East Campus - 3.8; North Campus - 2.7.	2b. Analysis of North Campus responses and telephone follow-up survey indicated need for more business courses at that location. These have been scheduled beginning next fall.
	3. The volume of instruction offered through electronic means will increase each year.	3a. The number of hours of instruction offered through compressed video will increase each year.	3a. 334 hours of compressed video presentations were held this calendar year compared to 327 in previous year.	3a. Further inquiry by staff revealed that courses conducted this year were not as appropriate for compressed video presentation. Adjusted course offerings to fit technology.
		3b. The number of students enrolled in courses conducted on the World Wide Web will increase 10% a year.	3b. 614 students were enrolled in WWW programs this year compared to 278 previous year.	3b. Rate of growth requires closer monitoring of equality of student achievement with traditional means of delivery.

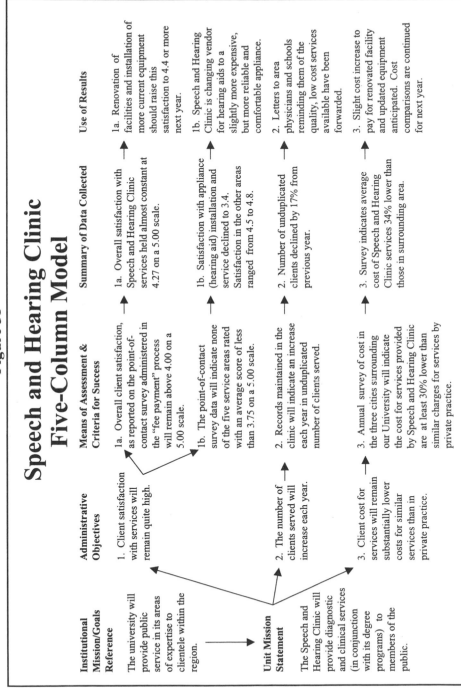

Figure 51

Speech and Hearing Clinic Five-Column Model

Institutional Mission/Goals Reference	Administrative Objectives	Means of Assessment & Criteria for Success	Summary of Data Collected	Use of Results
The university will provide public service in its areas of expertise to clientele within the region.	1. Client satisfaction with services will remain quite high.	1a. Overall client satisfaction, as reported on the point-of-contact survey administered in the "fee payment" process will remain above 4.00 on a 5.00 scale.	1a. Overall satisfaction with Speech and Hearing Clinic services held almost constant at 4.27 on a 5.00 scale.	1a. Renovation of facilities and installation of more current equipment should raise this satisfaction to 4.4 or more next year.
		1b. The point-of-contact survey data will indicate none of the five service areas rated with an average score of less than 3.75 on a 5.00 scale.	1b. Satisfaction with appliance (hearing aid) installation and service declined to 3.4. Satisfaction in the other areas ranged from 4.5 to 4.8.	1b. Speech and Hearing Clinic is changing vendor for hearing aids to a slightly more expensive, but more reliable and comfortable appliance.
Unit Mission Statement The Speech and Hearing Clinic will provide diagnostic and clinical services (in conjunction with its degree programs) to members of the public.	2. The number of clients served will increase each year.	2. Records maintained in the clinic will indicate an increase each year in unduplicated number of clients served.	2. Number of unduplicated clients declined by 17% from previous year.	2. Letters to area physicians and schools reminding them of the quality, low cost services available have been forwarded.
	3. Client cost for services will remain substantially lower costs for similar services than in private practice.	3. Annual survey of cost in the three cities surrounding our University will indicate the cost for services provided by Speech and Hearing Clinic are at least 30% lower than similar charges for services by private practice.	3. Survey indicates average cost of Speech and Hearing Clinic services 34% lower than those in surrounding area.	3. Slight cost increase to pay for renovated facility and updated equipment anticipated. Cost comparisons are continued for next year.

CHAPTER VII

CONCLUDING COMMENTS REGARDING ASSESSMENT IN ADMINISTRATIVE AND EDUCATIONAL SUPPORT UNITS

Like so many other matters within our institutions, successful implementation of assessment activities in administrative and educational support (AES) units is only possible based upon the efforts of unit leadership and staff. The AES unit head or director that already must accomplish so much in administering the unit now has one more responsibility–implementation of institutional effectiveness or assessment activities within the unit. While the central administration of the institution should surely provide the technical and logistical support services for assessment, these services can only facilitate the work that must be done in the institution's administrative and educational support units.

As you've read through this publication, you have undoubtedly begun to appreciate that some degree of effort will be involved in departmental implementation under any conditions. Several themes regarding the nature of the effort which you are about to put forth are repeated in various ways throughout this publication. These are:

- Make absolutely certain of what is being required of your AES unit and understand the implications of that requirement.
- Involve professional staff in identification of administrative objectives.
- Assessment activities in AES units are accomplishable without high levels of statistical skills or research expertise.
- Keep the entire process as simple as possible. It is far better to complete a relatively modest assessment plan, than to fail to complete a very sophisticated design requiring back-breaking effort in producing mountains of data.
- Use the results of the assessment conducted to improve your AES unit's services to its clients.

The bad news is that if you have been asked to read this publication, you probably have no choice within your institution as to whether or not to implement assessment activities in your administrative or educational support unit. The good news is twofold: First, what you're being asked to do (through the Three-Column Model) is accomplishable within a modest effort during the next few months. Second, results of your assessment effort can be utilized to genuinely improve the *services* provided by your administrative or educational support unit to the clients you serve.

As in many things in life, implementation is not an option, but a requirement. Whether we make it a burdensome chore or an opportunity to improve our unit and its services is up to each of us as we lead our AES units.

AES UNIT ASSESSMENT DOCUMENTATION INSTRUCTIONS AND FORMS

(also available at: www.iea-nich.com)

Instructions for Title Page (Form A)

- In the blank provided at the top of the page, *indicate the name of the unit/department submitting the report*. There should be one Assessment Record Book for each Administrative or Educational Support Unit at the institution.
- In the blank provided, *indicate the "Assessment Period Covered" by the report that follows*. This should be indicated in months and years. For example: July 2000 – June 2001.
- In the space provided, *enter the date the assessment report was forwarded to the assessment committee or individual responsible for assessment at the institution*. This will assist in identification of each iteration and potential refinement of the assessment report covering the same time period.
- In the blank provided, *enter the name of the individual who was responsible for the report*. In some cases an individual staff member in the unit has been identified to represent the AES unit in assessment matters and that person would sign the form, otherwise the unit director would sign the form.

Instructions for Linkage Page (Form B)

- The three blanks at the top of the page should have the *identical information provided on the title page (Form A)*.
- In the box identified as "Institutional Mission/Goals Reference," *enter all or a portion of the institutional mission or goals which is supported by the AES Unit submitting the report*.
- In the box containing "Administrative or Educational Support Unit Mission Statement," *enter a brief statement of the unit's mission*.
- In each of the blocks listed under "Intended Administrative Objectives," *enter one of the administrative objectives selected for assessment during the cycle cited above*. It is recommended that there be at least three of these administrative objectives and definitely no more than five.

Instructions for Administrative Objective Report Pages (Form C)

- You will have one Administrative Objective Report Page (Form C) for each Administrative Objective stated on Form B. Thus, if there are three "Administrative Objectives" listed on the Form B, there will be three Form Cs.
- The three blanks on the top of Form C will be *completed identically to those on Form B*.
- On your first Administrative Objective Report Page (Form C), in the box underneath "Intended Administrative or Educational Support Objective," *transfer the first*

administrative objective from Form B. On the second Form C, *transfer the second administrative objective from Form B into the box at the top of Form C,* and continue this process for all objectives.

- Complete the boxes under the "First Means of Assessment for Objective Identified Above" subsection according to the directions listed below.
    1. Means of Unit Assessment & Criteria for Success: *Describe the source of your assessment information.* (for example: unit records, graduating student survey, or report from an external agency). Based on the selected means of assessment, provide a criteria for success which answers the question: "If our unit is functioning the way we think it 'ought' to function, what will be our score on this means of assessment?"
    2. Summary of Assessment Data Collected: *Enter a brief summary of the data you collected from your assessment activities.* There should be enough data here to convince the reader that assessment has been done. Data should be reported in exact figures, not rounded. Make sure the data collected relates back to the administrative objective described in the first box.
    3. Use of Results to Improve Unit Services: *Describe how the unit used the information obtained from assessment activities* described in the "Means of Unit Assessment and Criteria for Success" block to improve the unit's services. This improvement needs to relate back to the administrative objective stated in the box at the top of the page. If the unit fails to meet its criteria for success, then this section is used to describe what actions the unit has taken to assure that the objective is met. Information in this block needs to be stated in past tense to indicate what changes *were* made.

- Complete the boxes under "Second Means of Assessment for Objectives Identified Above:" as you completed the "First Means of Assessment for Objective Identified Above."

ASSESSMENT RECORD FOR
DEPARTMENT/UNIT
OF

_____

(Name of Administrative or Educational Support Department/Unit)

_____   _____

(Assessment Period Covered)   **(Date Submitted)**

Submitted By: _____

(Unit Assessment Representative)

Form A-Title Page

ASSESSMENT RECORD FOR
DEPARTMENT/UNIT
OF

THE UNIVERSITY OF MISSISSIPPI CAREER CENTER
(Name of Administrative or Educational Support Department/Unit)

July 1, 2000–June 30, 2001   **August 1, 2000**
(Assessment Period Covered)   **(Date Submitted)**

Submitted By: _____
(Unit Assessment Representative)

Form A-Title Page

ASSESSMENT REPORT
FOR

_____

(Administrative or Educational Support Unit)

_____   _____

(Assessment Period Covered)   (Date Submitted)

Expanded Statement of Institutional Purpose Linkage:

Institutional Mission/Goal(s) Reference:

Administrative or Educational Support Unit Mission Statement:

Intended Administrative Objectives:

1.

2.

3.

4.

5.

Form B-Linkage Page

ASSESSMENT REPORT
FOR
CAREER CENTER

(Administrative or Educational Support Unit)

July 1, 2000 - June 30, 2001   **August 1, 2001**

(Assessment Period Covered)   **(Date Submitted)**

Expanded Statement of Institutional Purpose Linkage:

Institutional Mission/Goal(s) Reference: Goal 6-..The University will continue to develop leadership and to instill in its students a sense of justice, moral courage, and tolerance for the views of others improve admissions, academic and career placement counseling.

Administrative or Educational Support Unit Mission Statement:
The Purpose of the Career Center is to assist students in transition from academic to the world of work by preparing students for life after graduation. To assist students, the Career Center offers an array of services which include: career counseling; 3 classes for academic credit; workshops and seminars on career-related subjects: assistance with resume writing and interviewing; and opportunities for part-time jobs, internships and full-time jobs.

Intended Administrative Objectives:

1. Graduates will be satisfied with services provided by the Career Center.

2. Students will be aware of employment opportunities.

3. The number of opportunities for students to find employment will increase.

4.

5.

Form B-Linkage Page

ASSESSMENT REPORT
FOR

_____

(Administrative or Educational Support Unit)

_____   _____

(Assessment Period Covered)   **(Date Submitted)**

Intended Administrative or Educational Support Objective:

NOTE: There should be one Form C for each administrative objective listed on Form B. Administrative objective should be restated in the box immediately below and the administrative objective number entered in the blank spaces.

___

First Means of Assessment for Objective Identified Above:

___ **a.** Means of Unit Assessment & Criteria for Success:

___**a.** Summary of Assessment Data Collected:

___**a.** Use of Results to Improve Unit Services:

Second Means of Assessment for Objective Identified Above:

__**b.** Means of Unit Assessment & Criteria for Success:

__**b.** Summary of Assessment Data Collected:

___**b.** Use of Results to Improve Unit Services:

Form C-Administrative Objective Report Page

ASSESSMENT REPORT
FOR
CAREER CENTER
(Administrative or Educational Support Unit)

July 1, 2000 - June 30, 2001	August 1, 2001
(Assessment Period Covered)	**(Date Submitted)**

Intended Administrative or Educational Support Objective:

NOTE: There should be one Form C for each administrative objective listed on Form B. Administrative unit objective should be restated in the box immediately below and the administrative objective number entered in the blank spaces.

1. Graduates will be satisfied with services provided by the Career Center.

First Means of Assessment for Objective Identified Above:

1 a. Means of Unit Assessment & Criteria for Success: Respondents will indicate on graduating student survey an average rating of 3.4 or higher as to satisfaction with Career Center.

1a. Summary of Assessment Data Collected: Graduates rated satisfaction with Career Center as 3.4. However, the international students only gave a 1.4 satisfaction rating.

1a. Use of Results to Improve Unit Services : While criteria for success was met, workshops have been held by Career Center staff in conjunction with International Services to provide direct services to international students. Collecting material from University of Texas' program.

Second Means of Assessment for Objective Identified Above:

1b. Means of Unit Assessment & Criteria for Success: 95% of students completing a point-of-contact survey will be "very satisfied" or "satisfied" with their "overall experience with the Career Center." On no individual item (10 items) will more than 10% of students respond "dissatisfied" or "very dissatisfied".

1b. Summary of Assessment Data Collected: 63% of students responding to point of contact survey indicated satisfaction with "overall experience" with Career Center. Most dissatisfaction was expressed in availability of access to technical career sources (34%).

1b. Use of Results to Improve Unit Services: Career Center staff have located several new technical sources of career information. New work stations are being created using computer hardware donated by recruiting companies.

Form C-Administrative Objective Report Page

ASSESSMENT REPORT

FOR

CAREER CENTER

(Administrative or Educational Support Unit)

July 1, 2000-June30, 2001   **August 1, 2001**

(Assessment Period Covered)   **(Date Submitted)**

Intended Administrative or Educational Support Objective:

NOTE: There should be one Form C for each administrative objective listed on Form B. Administrative unit objective should be restated in the box immediately below and the administrative objective number entered in the blank spaces.

---

2. Students will be aware of employment opportunities.

First Means of Assessment for Objective Identified Above:

2a. Means of Unit Assessment & Criteria for Success: Records maintained will indicate an increase of 5% in number of job search workshops.

2a. Summary of Assessment Data Collected: There was a 9% increase in the number of job search workshops presented and an increase of 17% in the number of students attended the workshops.

2a. Use of Results to Improve Unit Services : Although the immediate goal was met last year the staff is continuing the level of job search workshops presented but want also to increase the number of classroom presentations on job search techniques for specific majors by 25%.

Means of Assessment for Objective Identified Above:

2b. Means of Unit Assessment & Criteria for Success: On the Alumni Survey given one year after graduation, graduates will indicate a 3.4 agreement to question: "The Career Center increased my awareness of employment opportunities in my field of study."

2b. Summary of Assessment Data Collected: Graduates on the Alumni survey indicated a 3.3 agreement to question: "The Career Center increased my awareness of employment opportunities in my field of study."

2b. Use of Results to Improve Unit Services: Staff is adding additional questions to the Alumni Survey to find out "where" students gained awareness of job opportunities.

Form C-Administrative Objective Report Page

ASSESSMENT REPORT
FOR
CAREER CENTER
(Administrative or Educational Support Unit)

July 1, 2000-June 30, 2001	August 1, 2001
(Assessment Period Covered)	(Date Submitted)

Intended Administrative or Educational Support Objective:

NOTE: There should be one Form C for each administrative objective listed on Form B. Administrative unit objective should be restated in the box immediately below and the administrative objective number entered in the blank spaces.

---

3. The number of opportunities for students to find employment will increase.

First Means of Assessment for Objective Identified Above:

3a. Means of Unit Assessment & Criteria for Success: Career Center records will indicate the number of resumes referred to employers will increase 24% over previous year.

3a. Summary of Assessment Data Collected: Number of resumes forwarded to employers was 9% over last year. Major decrease was in resumes for business and accounting majors.

3a. Use of Results to Improve Unit Services: Staff researched market and located 3 new internet resume sources for business, accounting and liberal arts majors.

Second Means of Assessment for Objective Identified Above:

3b. Means of Unit Assessment & Criteria for Success: Career Center records will indicate the number of companies attending "Job Fairs" will increase 10% over previous year.

3b. Summary of Assessment Data Collected: The number of companies attending"Job Fairs" last year increased from 141 in 1999-2000 to 173 in 2000-2001. However, companies coming for recruiting decreased 17%.

3b. Use of Results to Improve Unit Services: Staff survey of other institutions indicated this is a new trend. Career Center committee has been established to determine if this is leading to more job offers.

Form C-Administrative Objective Report Page

SUMMARY OF NATIONALLY STANDARDIZED ATTITUDINAL SURVEYS FOR ASSESSMENT IN HIGHER EDUCATION

American College Testing, the College Board in co-sponsorship with the National Center for Higher Education Management Systems (NCHEMS), as well as USA Group Noel Levitz, provide nationally standardized attitudinal surveys of students and alumni.

The American College Testing Program Evaluation Survey Services (ACT/ESS) offers fifteen post-secondary survey instruments covering the following subjects:

- Adult Learner Needs Assessment Survey
- Alumni Survey
- Alumni Survey (Two-Year College Form)
- Alumni Outcomes Survey
- College Outcomes Survey
- College Student Needs Assessment Survey
- Entering Student Survey
- Financial Aid Services Survey
- Student Opinion Survey
- Student Opinion Survey (Two-Year College Form)
- Survey of Academic Advising
- Survey of Current Activities and Plans
- Survey of Post-Secondary Plans
- Withdrawing/Non-Returning Student Survey
- Withdrawing/Non-Returning Student Survey (Short Form)

These surveys are optically scanned, containing two or four pages of questions designed for making general evaluations of the institution's services. Local personnel have the option of adding twenty to thirty additional questions for each of the surveys. ACT also offers a catalog of additional survey items which institutions may select from in lieu of writing their own questions. In addition, each instrument provides spaces for the participant to write comments or suggestions. This set of surveys has been in existence since 1979 and well over a million have been distributed on colleges and university campuses.

Of particular interest to administrative and educational support unit heads are the specific surveys concerning Financial Aid Services and Academic Advising as well as the Student Opinion Survey (both two- and four-year versions). The Student Opinion

Survey provides information concerning the use of and level of satisfaction with various campus services and programs as well as student satisfaction with the college environment, including the areas of admissions, rules and regulations, facilities, registration and general. Further information concerning the ESS Surveys may be gained by contacting:

Dr. David A. Lutz, Director
Post-Secondary Services
Outcomes Assessment
ACT
P.O. Box 168
Iowa City, Iowa 52243-0168
Phone: 319-337-1051
Internet: Lutz@ACT.org

The Student Outcomes Information Service (SOIS), co-sponsored by the College Board and the National Center for Higher Education Management Systems, is in many respects like the ACT/ESS. The questionnaires focus on six different points during and after college:

1. Entering student
2. Continuing student
3. Program completer and graduating student
4. Former student
5. Recent Alumnus
6. Three to five-year follow-up

The questionnaires, offered in formats for both two-year and four-year institutions, provide background demographics; survey educational experiences, plans, and goals; identify the need for, use of, and satisfaction with institutional services; and give perceptions and impressions of the institution as held by the various survey populations.

Perhaps the most significant difference between the SOIS and ACT families of surveys is the coordinated, research-oriented approach of the SOIS, which is supported by a carefully written handbook, *Student Outcomes Questionnaires: An Implementation Handbook* (2nd ed., 1983), by Peter T. Ewell.

Ewell takes the novice practitioner through the process step by step and carefully points out tricks and essential steps to help guarantee successful, usable survey results. As with ACT, data processing and questionnaire analyses are available. Annual summaries of information from participating institutions are also made available.

Information concerning the SOIS can be gained by contacting:

Dr. Peter T. Ewell, Senior Associate
National Center for Higher Education Management System
P.O. Drawer P
Boulder, CO 80301
Phone: 303-497-0371
E-mail: ewellp@colorado.edu

The Student Satisfaction Inventory from the USA Group Noel Levitz offers a sophisticated student satisfaction survey that determines student opinion concerning twelve scales:

- Campus climate
- Student centeredness
- Response of institution to diverse populations
- Safety and security
- Service excellence
- Concern for the individual
- Instruction
- Academic advising
- Recruitment
- Financial aid
- Registration
- Campus support services

Benchmark data are available for comparison by institutional type (two-year, four-year). Unlike some other instruments, the Student Satisfaction Inventory measures what's important to students, as well as how well they are satisfied. By measuring both satisfaction and importance, the inventory pinpoints students' perceptions more precisely regarding aspects of campus environment which are of particular student importance. This survey has been widely utilized in the student services sector and in conjunction with efforts to increase student retention. Further information concerning Student Satisfactory Inventory may be gained by contacting:

USA Group Noel Levitz
Noel Levitz Office Park
2101 ACT Circle
Iowa City, Iowa 52245-9581
Phone: 1-800-876-1117
Email: info@noellevitz.com

AVAILABILITY OF OPTICAL MARK READERS AND SOFTWARE TO PREPARE CUSTOMIZED ASSESSMENT SURVEYS

The primary vendors for the creation of locally developed assessment surveys are National Computer Systems, Inc., and Scantron Services Group. National Computer Systems, Inc., markets a series of optical mark readers known as OPSCAN which scan both pencil and pen. They feature a programmable interactive printer that prints information such as error codes, alpha-numeric messages, serial numbers, validation flags, and test scores based on data that is scanned with no effect on the processing rate. A half-inch magnetic tape drive is also available for data storage and the barcode attachment delivers immediate automatic barcode identification. The OPSCAN series of scanners is widely utilized on college and university campuses. Additional information is available at either 1-800-431-1421 or *www.ncs.com*.

Scantron Services Group markets a line of optical mark readers which is comprised of five scanners designed to collect data quickly and accurately. Scantron offers a wide variety of software packages and scanable documents that work together with each scan mark to assist in data collection or management task. All five optical mark readers offer automatic document feed, either as a standard feature or an option. This eliminates the need to hand feed documents to a scanner. Other options include an interactive printer, as well as ink and barcode reading capabilities. Of particular interest is their testing and assessment software for Windows® known as "PARSCORE" which is designed to support assessment implementation. Additional information concerning Scantron Services Group can be obtained at *www.scantron.com*

A very useful software package for utilization with optical mark recognition systems is the Bubble Publishing Suite. This suite of programs contains their Form Shop, Scan Shop, and Report Shop programs which enable the user to design the forms (surveys), scan them into a computer and provide a customized set of reports. It is compatible with a number of hardware configurations and any desktop OMR scanner. Additional information concerning the Bubble Publishing Suite may be identified at www.bubblepublishing.com.